D0444987

The POWER of
TALK

We dedicate this book to our past, present, and future students, whose enthusiasm helped inspire this book.

The POWER of TALK

How Words Change Our Lives

Felecia Briscoe
Gilberto Arriaza
Rosemary C. Henze

CORWIN
A SAGE Company

Copyright © 2009 by Felecia M. Briscoe, Gilberto Arriaza, Rosemary C. Henze

All rights reserved. When forms and sample documents are included, their use is authorized only by educators, local school sites, and/or noncommercial or nonprofit entities that have purchased the book. Except for that usage, no part of this book may be reproduced or utilized in any form or by any means, electronic or mechanical, including photocopying, recording, or by any information storage and retrieval system, without permission in writing from the publisher.

For information:

Corwin
A SAGE Company
2455 Teller Road
Thousand Oaks, California 91320
(800) 233-9936
Fax: (800) 417-2466
www.corwinpress.com

SAGE Ltd.
1 Oliver's Yard
55 City Road
London EC1Y 1SP
United Kingdom

SAGE India Pvt. Ltd.
B 1/I 1 Mohan Cooperative
 Industrial Area
Mathura Road,
 New Delhi 110 044
India

SAGE Asia-Pacific Pte. Ltd.
33 Pekin Street #02-01
Far East Square
Singapore 048763

Printed in the United States of America.

Library of Congress Cataloging-in-Publication Data

Briscoe, Felecia.
The power of talk : how words change our lives / Felecia Briscoe, Gilberto Arriaza, Rosemary C. Henze.
     p. cm.
Includes bibliographical references and index.
ISBN 978-1-4129-5601-7 (cloth)
ISBN 978-1-4129-5602-4 (pbk.)

     1. Discourse analysis—Social aspects. 2. Communication in education. 3. Language and education—Social aspects. 4. Sociolinguistics. 5. Equality. I. Arriaza, Gilberto. II. Henze, Rosemary C. III. Title.

P302.84.B74 2009
306.44—dc22   2008044777

This book is printed on acid-free paper.

09   10   11   12   13   10   9   8   7   6   5   4   3   2   1

Acquisitions Editor:	Arnis Burvikovs
Associate Editor:	Desirée A. Bartlett
Production Editor:	Eric Garner
Copy Editor:	Kathy Conde
Typesetter:	C&M Digitals (P) Ltd.
Proofreader:	Carole Quandt
Indexer:	Terri Corry
Cover Designer:	Anthony Paular

Contents

Acknowledgments

We thank and acknowledge the hardworking educators who freely gave of their time to share with us their experiences in the schools and Vanessa Kenon for her assistance in putting this book together. We would also like to express our appreciation for Arnis Burvikovs, Desirée A. Bartlett, and the rest of the staff at Corwin for all their help.

Corwin gratefully acknowledges the contributions of the following individuals:

Theresa Abodeeb-Gentile
Assistant Professor
University of Hartford
West Hartford, CT

David Callaway
Teacher
Carson Middle School
Fountain, CO

Michelle Drechsler
8th Grade Language Arts
  Teacher
Carson Middle School
Colorado Springs, CO

Karen L. Fernandez
English/Language Arts Coach
  and Teacher
Denver Center for International
  Studies
Denver, CO

Christine Landwehrle
5th-6th Grade Language Arts &
  Reading Teacher
Bedminster Township
  Public School
Bedminster, NJ

Melanie Mares
Academic Coach
Lowndes Middle School
Valdosta, GA

Masha Rudman
Professor
University of Massachusetts-
    Amherst
Amherst, MA

Lynn Atkinson Smolen
Professor
University of Akron
Akron, OH

C. Gordon Wells
Professor
University of California,
    Santa Cruz
Santa Cruz, CA

About the Authors

 **Felecia Briscoe**, an associate professor at UT San Antonio, earned her doctorate in educational foundations from the University of Cincinnati. She also has an MA in psychology with an emphasis in experimental cognitive psychology and a BS in elementary education with an emphasis in science from the University of Nevada, Las Vegas. Her research focuses on the relationship between power and knowledge. Her research interests are concerned with the development of educational equity especially as related to classism, racism, and sexism. She studies how power manifests in discourse. Her most recent article, published in *Journal for Critical Education Policy Studies* in 2006, is titled "Reproduction of Racialized Hierarchies: Ethnic Identities in the Discourse of Educational Leadership." She has also just completed a coauthored manuscript in which she analyzes the discourse of the U.S. legislation "No Child Left Behind." Dr. Briscoe has experienced a variety of teaching contexts. She started out as a seventh-grade science teacher in a public school in Las Vegas, Nevada. She also taught at the University of Cincinnati and at Concord College. She has been a member of the Educational Leadership and Policy Studies at the University of Texas, San Antonio, since the summer of 2000.

 **Gilberto Arriaza** graduated from the University of California, Berkeley, with a social and cultural focus on education. From 2000 to 2007, he taught at San Jose State University (SJSU) and is now a professor at California State University, East Bay's College of Education where he is the director of the Center for Leadership, Equity, and Research and chair of the department of educational leadership.

He has taught organizational theory, leadership, system analysis, school design, research methods, community involvement in schools, and advocacy for P–16 educators.

While at SJSU, Dr. Arriaza served as codirector of the Leading for Equity and Achievement Designs (LEAD) Center—focused on P–12 school reform. His work experience includes extensive research, leadership coaching, and school program evaluation. He has primarily worked for school districts, nonprofit organizations, and university institutions, including the Bay Area Coalition for Equitable Schools, California.

 **Rosemary C. Henze** is a professor in the Linguistics and Language Development Department at San José State University. Earlier, she worked for thirteen years in the nonprofit sector as a researcher and consultant in collaboration with K–12 public schools. Her interests center on the role of language in promoting educational equity, positive interethnic relations, and effective leadership. Recent publications include *Leading for Diversity: How School Leaders Promote Positive Interethnic Relations* (Corwin Press, 2002) and a video with the same title (Corwin Press, 2003); "Metaphors of Diversity, Intergroup Relations, and Equity in the Discourse of Educational Leadership" (*Journal of Language, Identity, and Education*, 2005); and *How Real Is Race? A Sourcebook on Race, Culture, and Biology* (Rowman & Littlefield Education, 2007). She received her doctorate in education with a minor in anthropology from Stanford University.

Introduction

Does our everyday use of language make a difference in the culture of schools, communities, workplaces, and society in general? The answer is, "Yes, yes, and yes!" This book addresses this issue and stresses how to use language to engender equity and social justice. The other question this book engages is, How does our use of language affect our understandings and the way we act? Through a series of vignettes and concrete examples, we show the complexity of the relationship between our speech and its impact on human organizations (e.g., schools)—speech that acts to reproduce present inequities and speech that is transforming.

WHY? THE SAME OLD PROBLEM

We wrote this book because, while there have already been volumes—whole libraries, in fact—written on the subject of school reform, one area remains relatively unexamined: the role of everyday language in the transformation of school culture.

For decades now, educators have been trying to make public schools in the United States truly embody democratic ideals. Fundamental to these ideals is the notion that schools should afford equitable and just access and outcomes to learning for all students; in other words, schooling should not reinforce or worsen existing inequities in our society based on ethnicity/race, class, gender, or other social dimensions. Countless well-intended efforts have not successfully transformed public education into an equitable and just system throughout the country. Where pockets of success exist, it has been difficult to replicate and spread the good news to other schools in other contexts.

1

Is there something reformers have been missing? A new reform strategy perhaps? A "silver bullet"? A new package designed to deliver better instruction, better curriculum, better assessment, better learning? Better leadership?

Recent research tells us that if there is any such thing, it will probably cost taxpayers and local communities bundles for new textbooks, new testing mechanisms, new technologies, and new staffing needs. Most educators have a "soft spot" for students, and anything that can be sold to us as doing a better job of educating them is immediately appealing. This book does not present a school reform package or any new and glitzy twist on instruction. Rather, we ask readers to reevaluate the power of the language they use on a daily basis in their work as educators and to consider a humble, no-tech, and yet extremely powerful intervention: changing our language to become more consistent in expressing our beliefs about equitable and socially just education.

WHAT? THE BOOK'S PURPOSE

This book is designed to help educators of all kinds become more skillful change agents by using language effectively as a tool for change. If we change our language we will probably also change what and how we think as well as what we do!

The changes involved require no new financial investment—only your time, your understanding, and the collective will to make them happen. We are not suggesting that language change alone can accomplish all that needs to be done to make schooling better. What we are saying is that language change is like a booster or amplifier (and sometimes the catalyst) that can assist educators in making the most of a concerted, coherent reform effort. Language is a largely unnoticed and unacknowledged tool that we are not yet using effectively. Changing the way we talk costs us no extra money yet has the potential to be extremely powerful in maximizing the changes we seek.

Edmundo Norte, one of the educators whose work we discuss in greater detail later on, says this about language:

It's pretty central. It's a key tool for trying to make change...because language reflects the way we frame and think about the world. One of the things I'm really explicit about in diversity trainings is not using language

> that represents the world as bipolar—either-or, good or bad, and how... language represents a way of conceptualizing and framing the world.... We participate in our own oppression by using language that supports a way of framing the world that is inherently going to lead to inequity—"There are going to be those that are smart and those that are dumb." So if you've got that basic framing down, then it becomes very easy for those who have the power—those who view themselves as right, or moral, to say they have the correct perspective and others don't. In the training I do, I'm very explicit about that.

When asked how people in the trainings react, he responded:

> It's one of the more powerful things, even though it's a stretch. People can recognize it in themselves—"Oh yeah, I do that." So I think people can connect both with how they do use it, and also make the link to seeing how it's not consistent with other values they express. So for example when I'm doing a training with teachers, I'll ask them, "What brought you into teaching? What was the vision that you had?" And when they name the different things, [they see that] ... if we're still thinking about the world in terms of either-or, right-wrong, good-bad, even if it's about the oppressor or the person in power, we're still buying into that system.

Educational leaders, teachers, and other school practitioners use language every day in a variety of social transactions: addressing conflicts, negotiating union contracts, developing a unified vision, contesting injustices, and so on. In each case the language used will either promote social justice or reproduce inequities. In terms of social actions, words and language are perhaps the most powerful force, as they are the primary means by which shared understandings are developed.

Language is largely taken for granted. We do not normally think about every word we say before we say it. Likewise, we do not carefully examine every word that is said to us. Anthropologist Clyde Kluckhohn once wrote, "It would hardly be the fish who would discover the existence of water."[1] This metaphor was originally used to describe the taken-for-granted nature of culture; it also easily applies to language. It is all around us, but for the most part, we do not have to think about it; we just use it. We even end up believing many of the assumptions and expectations conveyed implicitly through language, a fact that advertisers and politicians use to their advantage regularly.

Why not take hold of this amazing medium we use every day and put it to work in the service of creating a world that is more equitable and socially just?

How? Achieving the Purpose

As previously stated, our central purpose in writing this book is to help educators become more effective change agents in their quest to develop equitable and socially just schools. How do we plan to achieve this purpose? We do so by applying some of the analytical and creative skills of *critical discourse analysis* to everyday talk. We will explain this more fully in Chapter 1, but for now, suffice it to say that these skills involve becoming more aware of how language influences our beliefs and assumptions and also becoming knowledgeable about how we can use language to improve life circumstances in and out of schools.

Critical discourse analysis has been absent from the curriculum in most teacher preparation and educational leadership preparation programs. This approach is something quite different from political correctness. Most people are familiar with political correctness as a form of language change, but it has become merely symbolic to many people. Phrases such as "sanitation engineer" in place of "janitor" or "differently abled" in place of "handicapped" may show that one is a certain kind of person (e.g., liberal, progressive). A politically correct identity can also be used to put someone down as in "you're just being politically correct," or "I hate all that PC talk." Distancing oneself from the "PC" talkers signals an opposite identity as a "straight talker," someone who "tells it like it is," is "down to earth," and doesn't put "window dressings on the facts."

Norman Fairclough, in " 'Political Correctness': The Politics of Culture and Language"[2] points out that while it is liberals who have been labeled as PC, they are not the only ones who use relabeling and other language choices to help change perceptions and practices. In fact, marketing specialists use this tactic regularly when they relabel "bank accounts" as "financial products." So do politicians, when they relabel "learning" as "educational outcomes."

Transformations in language occur because we as individuals somehow come to consensus of what is wrong with language. When this social consensus converges with larger movements, such as the civil rights movement of the 1960s and 70s, then noticeable changes take place. One of the greatest successes has been in the area of gendered language. It is far more common in public discourse these days to hear *chair* or *chairperson* than the older form, *chairman*. And women have indeed taken their places in many of the leadership roles these terms express. But other changes have been far more superficial. What are some of the reasons for these rather limited effects?

For one thing, PC language has not always been interconnected with other actions, such as wage equity. Secondly, in many cases, people's beliefs and attitudes have not changed; they have merely adopted new or fashionable terms. Third, some efforts to spread PC language have been too "top down"; people do not appreciate having language changes forced on them by those in higher positions. In this regard, Fairclough points out that market strategists and politicians have actually been more successful at their language change efforts because they have not waged an overt campaign but rather used the implicit nature of culture and language to insert their changes. They haven't called attention to their language substitutions. And fourth, most of PC's focus has been on labels—nouns, noun phrases, and pronouns. PC language primarily affects the reference system of the language—the terms we use to talk about people. It hasn't done much to change the verbs or larger language structures we use.

So how does the approach we take in this book differ from PC language? First of all, we make connections across three dimensions: what people actually say, write, or sign; the context in which those words are used (e.g., to whom and in what setting the words are spoken); and the way those words connect to a larger belief system. By connecting these three dimensions to one another, we move beyond the superficial use of different words or labels.

Second, we believe that a coaching model is more appropriate to the goals of language change for equity than a top-down, monitoring model. We don't want to create a "language police force," and the best way to avoid this is to make language change an object of inquiry and cultural shift, not a forced hyperawareness that creates fear, shame, and inhibition, all of which act to shut down communication.

Third, we believe that while it is useful to look at the reference system (nouns, noun phrases, and pronouns) we use in our everyday language, it is also useful to look at other structures in our everyday language—for instance, the way we use metaphors, the ways in which we categorize people and activities, the verbs we use to express different activities, and the relative value or importance of the people and activities thus categorized. In sum, there are many aspects of language that we need to look at if we want to get a picture of how ideas about equity and social justice are encoded in language.

WHAT WILL YOU GET OUT OF THIS BOOK?

At a minimum, readers should take away the following enhancements in their repertoires as change agents:

1. An enhanced ability to recognize language that perpetuates or reinforces social inequities

2. An enhanced ability to use the power of language to interrupt cultural practices that perpetuate inequities

3. An enhanced ability to creatively seek and practice alternative language that more closely reflects equitable educational ideals

4. An enhanced ability to lead others in the practice of critical language awareness and transformative language use

In the next section we introduce ourselves and the experiences that have helped to develop our interest in social justice and language.

MORE ABOUT THE AUTHORS

What we do and who we are profoundly impacts our understanding of the world, which in turn influences our behaviors. Intellectual honesty plays a pivotal role in our work as researchers and as scholars. Thus, we write this note in order to disclose our lives as they intersect with this book's topic. Below, we have each written a brief description of our positionings in society as well as about some of the data sources from which we draw our illustrations in this book.[3]

Felecia Briscoe

I am an associate professor in the department of Educational Leadership and Policy Studies at the University of Texas. Although my ethnicity is quite mixed, European American (Irish) predominates and thus my appearance and experiences are largely that of a European American woman. I grew up on a family farm the third of eleven children in a very poor working-class family on the outskirts of Las Vegas, Nevada. I graduated high school as valedictorian, firmly believing that public education offered the only trustworthy path out of poverty. I married at the age of eighteen. Six years later, with three children, all under the age of five, I got divorced. At that time I had less than two years of college.

I then worked and completed a bachelor's degree in K–8 education with a science emphasis and a masters degree in psychology with an emphasis in experimental cognitive psychology. I spent the next four years as a teacher in the public schools as a middle school science teacher. After that I moved to Cincinnati and earned my doctorate in education with an emphasis in social foundations.

Three types of experiences have influenced me to become an advocate for social justice, especially in education. First, my experiences as a working-class woman, single with three children, working her way through college and graduate school helped me to understand that the academic playing field was indeed stacked against the working and poverty classes.

Second, as I began to associate with more middle-class people in graduate school I came to understand that their public school (and private school) experiences were *very* different from mine and that they had been much better prepared for selecting and attending college. These middle-class people know about things like the Merit Scholarships that were completely out of the purview of my teachers and my family when I was growing up. I understood therefore that U.S. public schools were not providing equal distributions of knowledge and educational opportunities for all children.

My third experience was as a public school science teacher. While I was teaching, the district decided that children hitherto classified as special education were to be mainstreamed as much as possible into classes. The effect was that five African American boys suddenly appeared in my seventh-grade science classes. From my interactions with these children, I could not see any indication that they suffered from any sort of mental deficit. I was upset by the fact that because they had spent years in special education, their reading skills were marginal at best. I went to the principal and asked how I was to give the boys a fair chance to succeed in my science class and at the same time to uphold high standards of learning.

The principal threw up his hands helplessly and said, "Do the best that you can."

I was horrified! I was being forced to be complicit in setting up these boys for failure. I would either have to fudge their grades saying that they had learned seventh grade science sufficiently to earn a passing grade, when in fact they had not and were not prepared for success at the next level of science; or I would have to fail them according to the standards that I had set up for the rest of the class. By the end of the semester, the boys could read much better than they could when they started, but their science learning was still considerably below average.

The fact that all the children who were mainstreamed into my class were African American boys made it vividly real to me that racism was not only alive, but that it had in fact been institutionalized. This teaching experience coupled with my experiences as a student and parent convinced me that our system of schooling did *not* operate in the best interests of all students. Since that time, I have been committed to gaining the understanding necessary to change our schooling system into a more just one.

The illustrations I use in this book were taken from many different sources. However, the majority comes from interviews with twenty-two educational leaders, conducted during the years 2005–2007 in a very large metropolitan city in Texas. The interviews were structured around six questions that addressed their perceptions of the strengths and weakness of our current schooling practices.[4] (Chapter 5 gives more details on this research.)

Gilberto Arriaza

I was born and raised in Guatemala. In 1982, I became part of the Central American Diaspora: For the first time in recent history, Central Americans from Guatemala, El Salvador, Nicaragua, and Honduras were forced out of the region as a result of a war between the dictatorial regimes of those days and the organized people. I was then, as I am now, an educator deeply committed to advancing social justice.

In a sense, this book captures issues that I—literally and symbolically—live with on a daily basis. My life experience in my new, adoptive country has been deeply transforming. Upon arrival, I was immediately labeled in terms of culture, phenotype, and language, which translates as Latino, brown, second-language speaker.

The options for me, then, were to be colonized by these labels or adopt these labels as sources of power. I took the latter option.

In 1982, I didn't speak English or understand the culture. I couldn't validate my formal education either. So I had to work from scratch: I went to a local community college to learn both the language and the education traditions of the United States. I later graduated from a state university with a BA first and a MA and teaching credentials later on, and I wound up completing a PhD at the University of California at Berkeley.

Today, I clearly know and understand the multiple ramifications of the cultural, racial, and linguistic descriptors that have been applied to me. They anchor my professional commitments in a way I truly doubt would have been possible in Guatemala. As M. M. Bakhtin has explained in his book, *The Dialogic Imagination*—in order to understand, I had to leave, so that I could see from a distance the place I had been. I practice this as often as I can afford to so as to "see" the United States, especially California.

Over the past four years, I followed a team of educators who had taken some courses from me when I taught at San José State University. To avoid conflict of interest and reduce bias, I conducted a study after they had graduated from the university. This study included a focus group from a population of twenty-seven educators. Other methodological details can be found in the text of this book.

Rosemary Henze

I grew up in Southern California in a situation that was clearly privileged compared to my two coauthors. One could say that my life so far has in large part been shaped by my slow journey of intentional downward mobility followed by an upswing again through education. My father immigrated to the United States from Austria at the age of thirty, and my mother was the daughter of a wealthy Chicago family, with mainly Danish and English ancestry.

I attended private schools through high school and was largely unaware of how privileged I was. My biggest awakening to issues of social justice happened after I finished my BA in art (from UC Santa Cruz) and went to work in a retail and wholesale art supply store in San Francisco. Working in the warehouse with men of diverse backgrounds who belonged to the Teamsters Union, I started to understand how prejudice and racism work. These were the very men I would have been frightened of before because of their "tough" looks and behaviors—and yet, through many conversations, I developed not only respect but also friendships with them. Through constant questioning and self reflection, I gradually revised my stereotypes of working-class, Black, Latino, and White males.

In my late twenties, I moved toward education as a career path, first getting a master's degree in teaching English as a second language, and then after a few years of teaching ESL, going for my doctorate in education at Stanford University. It was at this time that I encountered social inequality as an intellectual area of study for the first time, enabling me to attach theories to what I had seen and experienced in my earlier jobs.

After I finished my doctorate, I worked for fourteen years in a nonprofit organization in Oakland, California, collaborating with schools to improve services in the area of bilingual and antiracist programs. I learned skills of project leadership, budget management, and grant writing, but most of all I learned how hard teachers work. Yet I also remember how demoralized and invisible I felt when people at academic conferences would look past my nametag with its nonacademic affiliation, quickly moving on to find someone more important to talk to. I was keenly aware that in the hierarchy of academia, where I was at the lower end of the social strata because I did not work in a university or even a two- or four-year college; the work I did in schools was seen as "practical" and "applied"—terms which in that context connote lower prestige.

Yet despite this and other experiences of feeling ignored or trivialized, there is no doubt that being a white woman raised in privileged circumstances has given me advantages many of my friends and colleagues have never had. Rather than feeling guilty and disabled about this, I have tried to turn my advantages into action by teaching, and by serving as a mentor to two girls through Big Brothers and Big Sisters. They have provided me with more lessons on the deep scars left by poverty, racism, sexism, and drug abuse. In these relationships, I struggle as all parents do with how to set boundaries in ways that will enable them to grow and flourish.

In constructing the examples for this book, I drew on a large database of interviews and observations with educators in twenty-one U.S. schools that were part of the "Leading for Diversity" research project, completed between 1996 and 1999.[5] Second, in 2007 I conducted interviews and observations specifically for this book with several educators in the Bay Area. In the book, you will find excerpts from three of these individuals: One is a director of curriculum and professional development for two charter schools; another is a director of a cross-cultural center on a college campus; and the third is a high school teacher-leader.

AVOIDING THE MASTER'S LANGUAGE TOOLS

As we wrote this book, we frequently talked about our own discourse. We critiqued our writing to try to make sure that we did not inadvertently use language that promoted inequities. One of the issues we struggled with was how to describe the various social groups that we discuss in this book. We decided that if we knew how people referred to themselves, we should use that category for that person. We also decided that when possible, we would try to avoid terms of color (which promote a biological understanding of differences) but instead use terms of ethnicity. Ethnicity is a more specific social category that avoids reinforcing the scientifically invalid notion of separate, biologically-different "races."[6] Also, if we quoted from a study, we used the same terms as those used in the study.

Our early struggles over chapter titles provide another illustration of how we interrogated our own use of language and tried to guard against the tendency to replicate what we hoped to change. Our initial chapter titles were one-word constructions such as "Othering," "Disappearing," and "Stratifying." While we liked the simplicity of these titles, we began to question whether they really communicated our intent, which was to not only enhance readers' awareness of what NOT to do but also to suggest alternatives—to use, in Paolo Friere's translated words, a "language of possibility" and to emphasize transformation. Thus, we eventually came to the resolution you see in most of our present chapter titles—an emphasis on positive, alternative practices.

OVERVIEW OF THE CHAPTERS

For those who are interested in a specific topic or want to see the way the book unfolds we provide a brief overview of each of the chapters.

Chapter 1: "The Power of Language: A Medium for Promoting Social Justice and Equity" lays the groundwork. Most of the major concepts used throughout the book are introduced and explained here.

Chapter 2: "Becoming Effective in Using Critical Language Awareness" describes habits and strategies that will help change agents work with others.

Chapter 3: "Avoiding Othering: Practicing Inclusion" defines and presents examples of "othering" language. In it we explain how all too often, othering polarizes discussions and creates in- and out-groups.

Chapter 4: "Disrupting Prejudice: A Communicative Approach" proposes language skills and strategies for moving away from the dehumanizing focus on data, numbers, and percentages of whole groups at the expense of the individual.

Chapter 5: "Exceptionalizing or Democratizing?" provides examples of exceptionalizing language and how to recognize it. It also provides suggestions for avoiding exceptionalizing and developing discourses of equity.

Chapter 6: "Recognizing and Revising Stratifying Discourse" suggests language patterns that move away from reproducing hierarchies and toward more egalitarian ways of understanding ourselves and others.

Chapter 7: "Contesting Deficit Labels" offers a set of communication skills for redressing the impact of labeling. These communication skills are crafted so as to invite others to think about the way they talk, rather than to blame or shame others.

Chapter 8: "Conclusion: The Power of Talk" brings together all themes, concepts, and skills, summing up the book, suggesting ways in which this knowledge could be used, and presenting some final thoughts about why we believe this book to be an important topic for both schools and society.

WHERE AND WHEN MIGHT THE BOOK BE USED?

In addition to individual reading, we hope that this book may be used in a variety of group settings. For example, a group of people at your school or higher education institution could read it together, do the activities and hold discussions after each chapter.

In higher education, the book could be part of the curriculum in a teacher education or leadership preparation program—either as a separate course or as part of a course that deals with leadership and change, equity, social justice, multicultural education, or other related themes. It could also be used in college and university courses that deal with critical thinking, communication, linguistics, and any of the behavioral sciences including anthropology, sociology, and psychology.

Many sections of the book could also be used for high school students in a language class such as English, journalism, or critical thinking. Consultants who do diversity and communication training in schools and businesses might also find this book useful because a large part of what they do is assist people in communicating more effectively in their workplace.

NOTES

1. Kluckhohn, C. (1959). *Mirror for man,* p. 16.
2. Fairclough, N. (2003).
3. We three met at a panel discussion at the American Anthropological Association Conference in Chicago in 2003.
4. The educational leaders who participated included: a Black American (this is how the participant described himself), eight Latinas/os, and thirteen Euro-Americans. The thirteen women and nine men who participated ranged between the ages of thirty-six and fifty-five. Eleven of these interviews were with educational leaders who worked in the three highest income school districts of the city and eleven of them were from three lowest income school districts.
5. Henze, Katz, Norte, Sather, and Walker (2002).
6. Mukhopadhyay, Henze, and Moses (2007).

CHAPTER ONE

The Power of Language

A Medium for Promoting Social Justice and Equity

In this chapter, we explain the grounding ideas of this book, including key concepts such as *social justice*, *language of possibility*, and others; we hope to establish a shared understanding of these ideas and concepts and their associated words. This is especially important because many of these terms vary in their interpretation. Our intent is to be as transparent as possible with meanings and to model what we advocate throughout the book.

IN WHAT WAYS IS LANGUAGE A TRANSFORMATIVE FORCE IN SOCIETY?

For reflection: To what extent are you aware of your language use in everyday interactions? Do you monitor yourself carefully, or do you speak spontaneously? What factors in the social situation tend to make you monitor your language more?

The idea that language can be a "trigger for broader social change"[1] has been around for a long time. Yet surprisingly, it rarely shows up in preparation and inservice programs for teachers and educational leaders. In this book, we place this idea at the very center of what educators in a democratic society do on an everyday basis. Every day, proactive educators try to make their educational institutions healthy, positive environments that challenge all students to develop their skills, knowledge, and ability to relate positively to others. They also attempt to right the effects of past injustices and to intervene in present ones. None of these actions would be possible without language. Educators use language to communicate their expectations of students, faculty, and parents; to discuss policies, praise people, propose changes in curriculum, indicate that they are listening, carry out disciplinary action, and for a host of other actions. Whether spoken, written, or signed, language is the medium through which educational leaders make their intentions known to others. Everyone who plays a formal or informal leadership role in education—including teachers, principals, school board members, community leaders—uses language as a medium for their actions; however, when speaking spontaneously, we usually don't have time to think carefully about *how* we say things. We just hope that our words come out more or less they way we intended.

Yet by moving toward a greater awareness of language, we can in fact use language to embody changes we believe in. Language embodies a potential for change when it is linked to larger social forces. In the United States, changes in the names of ethnoracial groups co-occurred with civil rights action and a movement away from a classification system based on skin color (black, yellow, brown, white) that was used to justify a social hierarchy based on race; "African American," "Asian American," and other ethnoracial labels became part of everyday discourse in the 1960s along with demands for equal rights and recognition. The shift in language from *Black* to *African American* was significant because it moved from an emphasis on skin color (a racialized feature) to a dual emphasis on origin (African) and current nationality (U.S. American).[2] As a society of mostly immigrants, we now have available language that tells us something about people's ancestry, a more meaningful piece of information than skin color, which in any so-called racial group always ranged along a broad continuum anyway. It is also helpful to include *American* because a visiting professional from Korea may have little in common with a third- or fourth-generation Korean American.

The case of Guatemala's Maya people also illustrates this point. When European explorers in 1492 mistakenly thought they had landed in India, they dubbed the local people they encountered "Indians." This label not only connoted the wrong continent but was also used as a derogatory, demeaning name to distinguish those claiming European lineage (who tend to be of lighter complexion) from those of more indigenous heritage (who tend to be of darker complexion). In the 1980s, the indigenous people of Guatemala began to systematically assert the right for a name disassociated with such baggage. The struggle to adopt the name *Maya* was linked to a broader struggle for basic civil and political rights. Currently, the use of Maya for people of indigenous heritage has become widespread in that country, and at the same time, the Maya have claimed other rights.[3]

1. The Relationship Between Language and Thought

For reflection: Think of a time when you realized that you saw the world differently from someone who spoke a different first language than you. What was the difference? Do you think your first language was involved in structuring these different ways of thinking? How much freedom do we have to think outside of the structures and words our first language provides?

To understand how changing language shapes our thinking, we need to go back a bit in history to consider the claim made in the 1940s by Edward Sapir, a linguist, and Benjamin Whorf, a fire insurance salesman who was a student of Sapir's. They developed the idea that the language we use actually determines the way we think.[4] What they meant is that speakers of different languages actually think differently, due to the differences in the way languages express actions, things, and so on. For example, the Hopi language, unlike English, expresses many concepts related to nature as movements (actions) rather than static entities. In Hopi, one cannot talk about a wave as a thing; one can only talk about the motion it produces, using a verb that roughly translates in English as "waving." Sapir and Whorf's theoretical claim was that underlying structural and semantic differences among languages lay down certain thought patterns early in childhood. Hopi speakers, they claimed, are likely to think more in terms of action and motion than English speakers— who for their part tend to think more in terms of things.

This claim that our language determines our thought patterns became known as the "strong form" of Sapir and Whorf's hypothesis, and it led to the corollary that people are like prisoners of their language. They cannot ever really acquire the thinking patterns of another language.[5] But as you might imagine, there were many challenges to this claim, in part because people can and do acquire other languages and in many instances do learn to think in the new language. In multilingual societies, it is normal to speak more than two languages from early childhood onward. Paraguay is one of many such cases. There, inhabitants speak Spanish and Guarani languages nationally, as well as a local variety of Spanish that is mixed with Guarani, even though the indigenous Guarani people no longer exist as a distinctive community. If language absolutely determined the way we think, we wouldn't be able to translate from one language to another. Granted, there will always be concepts which are difficult or even impossible to translate. But by and large, professional translators do a remarkable job.

Most linguists these days accept a modified version of Sapir and Whorf's theoretical claim. Instead of saying that our primary language *determines* the way we think, the modified version says that our primary language (or languages, in the case of childhood bilinguals) *shapes* or *influences* the way we think.

2. Language Reflects Existing Cultural and Physical Realities

For reflection: In what ways does your school categorize students? Do all schools you know of use the same categorization system as yours? Are different systems used by students versus faculty and staff? How can you explain the differences in categorization, if any?

Most of us can readily accept the notion that language reflects (or expresses) our cultural and physical reality. After all, one of the functions of language is to enable us to talk about the things of our world and the actions we perform in it. So, for example, if it is important for us to distinguish among different types of rocks, our language develops ways to express those distinctions. We can talk about differences that reflect the substance of the rock, such as granite versus marble; the size and shape of the rock, such as pebbles versus boulders; and so on. Eskimo languages make, for instance, fine distinctions among many different kinds of snow, obviously reflecting the need for people in the arctic environment to describe distinctions that make a difference in hunting prospects, travel conditions, and other activities that are contingent on the weather. Such distinctions would not be so important to people living in a warm, urban environment; therefore, a more limited number of snow words are adequate.[6]

In a school environment, we have words not only for the things that are important in that environment—such as desks, whiteboards, and computers—but also for classifications of people such as students, teachers, administrators, and so on. Many of these seem natural—they have been ingrained in us since childhood, so much so that it is difficult to think about schools without these categories of objects and people.

3. Language Also Constructs Our Cultural Realities

It is somewhat more difficult to accept the notion that we *construct* our world through language. In other words, language doesn't just reflect or express what is already there, like the kinds of rocks or snow in our environment. It also enables us to create categories, labels, and relationships that are different from the ones used by people in other cultures—or even people who to a large degree share our culture!

We see this variation when we look at kinship systems around the world. In English, the word *uncle* denotes any of a number of different relationships. An uncle can be the father's brother, the mother's brother, the husband of the father's sister, the husband of the mother's sister, and even sometimes an unrelated person like "Uncle Sam." It's not that English speakers can't express or understand these differences—obviously, we just did! But it took us longer; we had to use more words to say it. In Chinese and many other languages, each of these specific relationships has its own special term. In most Latin American societies, on the other hand, an uncle or aunt can simply be an intimate, close friend to the father or mother. This type of uncle or aunt has somewhat less moral responsibility toward the niece or nephew than blood-related uncles and aunts.

Why does this variation exist? Anthropologists argue that in Chinese, different roles, responsibilities, and privileges are accorded to different types of "uncles." Therefore, it's important to make the specific relationship overt, and what better way than to give each relationship its own label? An English speaker raised without this particular kinship system can understand the basic relationships in terms of biological lineage and whether the relationship is on the father's or the mother's side. But the same

English speaker, unless it has been spelled out, will not understand the system of roles, responsibilities, and privileges associated with each of the terms for uncle that the Chinese speaker grew up with. In sum, the English language concept of "uncle" doesn't map exactly onto the Chinese concept.

How does this relate to constructing our world through language? The example from different kinship systems demonstrates that when it comes to social relationships, cultures vary in the ways they classify family members. This variation tells us that there is nothing fixed about the way we classify relatives. It is only through custom and tradition that kinship terms become fixed in their meaning. When we travel or live in another culture, we come to realize that these meanings are only customary in our own culture, and the shifting nature of language and its connection to "reality" becomes evident.

We've established so far that the language we use shapes or influences how we think about the world. But so far, we've been talking about very different languages, like Hopi versus English, Spanish versus Guarani, and Chinese versus English.

4. Making Changes Within the Same Language

For reflection: What happens if we make small adjustments in the words we use to communicate with people who share our language? Have you ever tried to change the way you refer to certain groups of people? How did it work out? Did you feel the change better reflected your intentions? Or were you just doing it to be "politically correct"?

Here, we consider three examples:

1. *Getting rid of gender bias:* In the 1960s, feminists began to encourage writers to use nonsexist language. Among other changes, writers were urged to stop using the masculine pronoun *he* as the generic pronoun (when they really mean he *or* she). Instead, they started consciously using *she or he* (alternating the masculine and feminine pronouns, or using *they* instead) because they wanted to signify that the male pronoun was not automatically privileged as a default for signifying both men and women; they wanted their language to reflect women's agency and participation in all spheres of life.

At the time, many people thought that this small shift in language use by a few individuals couldn't possibly change anything; it seemed so trivial. Even today, there are people who think these changes are just "window dressing." But looking at this situation more carefully, one can argue that this is exactly the sort of change that *did* develop into something broader. Making the English language less male-centered was part of a broad social movement. This little change was connected to lots of other little as well as bigger changes; people such as Simone de Beauvoir, Betty Friedan, Germaine Greer, and many others were working hard to advance women's economic and political power in the United States and other countries. Doing so involved not only empowering women; it also meant calling attention to the subtle ways in which we assume male privilege, and language was one very tangible way to see and hear those assumptions, which in English were manifested in terms like *chairman* and *policeman*, as well as the generic pronoun *he*.

While language changes by themselves were not responsible for the changes that came about in society as a result of the women's movement, they were part of the package. Language changes helped usher in a different consciousness, creating an awareness of how male privilege was taken for granted—men made more money than women and held more decision-making power in matters of foreign policy, the legal system, and other arenas. So language changes were a transformative force, absolutely necessary for changes to take hold, but not sufficient by themselves. They had to be linked with other actions, such as policy changes in companies regarding equal pay for equal work, establishment of publicly supported day care centers, and so on.

2. *Minding our metaphors:* According to George Lakoff, a cognitive linguist at the University of California, Berkeley, "Thinking differently requires speaking differently."[7] For the past couple of decades, Lakoff has been studying the way common everyday metaphors "frame" or inform our perceptions of social reality.[8] For example, in his 2004 book *Don't Think of an Elephant,* he discusses the metaphor behind the phrase "tax relief." Usually when we use the word *relief*, we are referring to relief from some type of illness or affliction. Taxes in this phrase are framed as an affliction that requires us to seek relief (in the form of lowered taxes). Anyone who lowers taxes (thereby reducing the affliction) is viewed as a hero or

heroine. Anyone who opposes the lowering of taxes is seen as a villain.

Imagine, however, that we use a different metaphor—and therefore, a different frame. Instead of seeing taxes as an affliction, we use the metaphor of taxes as membership dues. Everybody who lives in the United States is a member and, as such, receives many benefits—public transportation system, public schools, public health, police, and so on. Like a member of any club, we pay dues for that membership. This shift of metaphors, says Lakoff, can affect the way people think about taxes.

Another person who has studied the use of metaphors is Otto Santa Ana, author of the 2002 book *Brown Tide Rising*. In this book, Santa Ana documents the use of metaphors for Latinos in the *Los Angeles Times* over a ten-year period. The most dominant metaphor for Latinos, he finds, is that of a flood or rising tide that spreads and inundates the land—in other words, a disaster (as in "a flood of new immigrants is impacting our city"). He argues, as does Lakoff, that these images trigger conceptual frames or sets of related associations that negatively affect the way we perceive Latinos. A flood evokes a deluge that spreads uncontrollably, destroys the land, and causes residents to flee for higher ground. Framing Latino immigrants in this way leads to negative feelings about all Latinos. Santa Ana suggests that a different metaphor, that of enrichment and productivity, would send a much more positive message. For example, "In the American Southwest, the immigrant stream makes the desert bloom."[9] Here, the metaphor of water is used in a positive sense as a giver of life and enabler of human activity.

3. *Changing language in education:* The same type of changes we have discussed above can be applied to education. Herve Varenne, an educational anthropologist, wrote in 1978 about a new principal at a high school who sent a memo to teachers a few weeks after his arrival at the school. The memo, which infuriated the teachers, started off as follows:

There is something intriguing about a teacher surplus which now exists in our country today. It permits us to be very selective in education. It enables us to assign teachers better. It even lets us replace some teachers we should not have hired in the first place. Possibly, at long last, it can stimulate us to be serious about individualizing education.[10]

It's easy to see why the teachers were infuriated. Not only were they cast as dispensable objects, like products in the marketplace that are overproduced, but they were also implicitly excluded from the "we/us" group with whom the speaker identified himself. The teachers were not seen as active agents in any of these sentences, only as passive recipients of the actions of the we/us group (presumably administrators).

Now let's look at a contrasting example to see how a more collaborative leader described the work of teachers and parents. In this excerpt from an interview, Mark Waters[11] is talking about the planning that went into the Chinese language program at his bilingual elementary school:

> They [teachers and parents] reached some wonderful accommodations and plans that one brain could never have come up with, but five brains could figure it out, and that's one of the hallmarks of what happens here—that everybody gets their oar in the water and keeps paddling until we figure out how we're going to get it going in the same direction, and it works.[12]

In this excerpt, teachers and parents are cast as active agents. Waters used the metaphor of paddling a canoe to depict their collaborative effort, and he included himself as one of the "paddlers."

These two examples suggest some of the language choices that are available to educational leaders. By using us/them constructions consistently (as in the first excerpt), a leader polarizes the situation, both reinforcing differences that may really exist, and at the same time constructing an even stronger line of separation between the in-group (us) and the out-group (them). If an educational leader uses this polarizing discourse regularly, it becomes *normalized*— meaning that most people simply assume that this is the way things are, without reflecting on why or how, or if things could be different. Furthermore, when an educator consistently puts a certain group of people in a passive position, as receivers of actions by other people, the educator implicitly takes away the possibility of the passively framed group acting as agents.

On the other hand, if an educator consistently describes the school community as an inclusive "we" or as people engaged in a dialogue or a joint project (e.g., paddling a canoe together), then the focus shifts toward understanding, communication, and shared goals, with everyone having an active role to play. Of course, other behavioral and institutional changes have to be consistent with this small change in language; otherwise, the change in language is merely a trivial attempt to be politically correct or to "sound inclusive" while still continuing to act in other ways to polarize the community.

5. Toward a Language of Possibility

For reflection: Do you ever invent new words or phrases instead of using language that you think is demeaning or contrary to your goals as an educator? Make a list of any such words or phrases. What were you trying to show or do by using them? Do you think you achieved the effect you desired?

It is one thing to critique existing language as sexist, ethnocentric, racist, classist, and so on but entirely another thing to offer constructive alternatives. In our personal lives, we all know people who are good at telling us what *not* to do but seldom offer suggestions for what *to* do.

Critique is necessary as a first step in social change. But an important element of critique is that we say what is wrong *and* offer suggestions for improvement. Being critical is not only being negative; a critical friend also gives you positive feedback and suggests what you might do to improve. Language becomes transformative when it offers alternatives to the status quo and incorporates them into ways of thinking and discourse, thereby carving out new or different categories, relationships, and ways of representing the world, and opening up the possibility of transformative practices.

Paolo Friere, a Brazilian educator who is known for the development of critical pedagogy,[13] introduced the term "language of possibility," which has been taken up by many others in slightly different forms. Otto Santa Ana, noted earlier in this chapter, speaks of the need to create "insubordinate metaphors to produce more inclusive American values, and more just practices for a new society."[14] The use of a language of possibility is embodied in the efforts we described earlier—the claiming of a higher status name by the Maya of Guatemala, removing male privilege and inserting gender neutral terms, portraying immigrant Latinos in California as enriching rather than inundating the land, and using inclusive rather than polarizing language in education.

When critique of existing language and instances of language of possibility are tied in a systematic, coherent way to a larger social movement, then we can say that *language is being used as a transformative force*. In other words, people recognize and use the power of language to shape and change our existing systems, be they social policies, education, environmental practices, health care, or other domains. The guiding question for us in this book is, "How can we use the transformative power of language to advance educational equity and social justice?"

We next turn to the meanings of these very terms—educational equity and social justice.

WHAT ARE EDUCATIONAL EQUITY AND SOCIAL JUSTICE?

So far, we have suggested that educational leaders ought to use language as a medium for transforming the status quo. But this can lead to the dangerous conclusion that all transformations are equally desirable or that change should happen for the sake of change.

Rather than seeking change blindly, we believe educators need to have a vision of what they are aiming toward. This vision has to incorporate values; education is never a value-free enterprise. Even the teacher who claims to teach "only the facts" is a purveyor of values, choosing not only *what* content to teach and what to leave out of the curriculum but also *how* to teach (e.g., instructional approaches can convey a value of individualism, collaboration, or competition). Of course, in certain eras, such as the current era of high stakes testing, teachers become more constrained in what they can teach and how they teach it. They still make choices, but those choices narrow or widen depending on the political and legal conditions of the time. And the political and legal decisions that affect education also promote or discourage certain values.

In this book, we openly advocate for educational transformation that aims toward equity and social justice.

1. Equity Versus Equality

For reflection: What do the words equity and equality mean to you? Write down the understandings you have now. After reading this section, did your understanding change?

Unlike the notion of *equality,* which presumes that the solution to academic and social inequities is to treat everyone equally, providing the same books, teachers, schools, and curriculum to all students, the notion of *equity* assumes that the "playing field" is not level, and therefore resources must be allocated differently according to the different places students find themselves at. All students start out at different points depending on how they are positioned in terms of socioeconomic class, racial category, language, gender, cultural background, family structure, and other variables that affect both individuals and families.

In an *equity-based approach,* institutional actions are designed to redress social, cultural, linguistic, and other differences. These actions might include, for example, summer programs to help students "catch up" before they enter ninth grade or English as a second language (ESL) programs that help immigrants acquire the language of instruction so that they can learn in English as soon as possible, while nurturing their native tongue. Equity can be applied to gender gaps, economic gaps, or any other group disparities in educational outcomes created by social injustices. Equity-based approaches are controversial, however, because some students receive resources not given to all students. This raises questions about fundamental ideas of fairness (understood as everybody getting exactly the same things) that are deeply embedded in U.S. belief systems. However, an equity-based approach argues that "fairness" has to be seen in a larger perspective. A teacher in a staff development workshop made the following analogy: "Everyone gets a pen, but maybe some people need help using that pen because they have only used pencils before."

In sum, we are defining equity as the necessary actions educators must take to bring out the potentials of all students regardless of their positioning (e.g., social, economic, gender, race, sexuality) so that in the end all groups of children are able to produce equally high academic results. However, we recognize, as Thea Abu El-Haj writes, that this definition of equity, by focusing on academic outcomes, fails to question "the apparent neutrality of the goods that are being distributed."[15] The next section addresses this issue.

2. Social Justice

For reflection: What does "social justice" mean to you? Write down your understanding. After reading this section, has your understanding changed?

Lindsay, Robins, and Terrell, who wrote a book for school leaders titled *Cultural Proficiency: A Manual for School Leaders,* defined *social justice* as "activism to rectify inequitable distribution of resources, such as nutrition, prenatal care, child care, and early childhood education."[16] This quote suggests that social justice is closely tied to equity, and in fact, as Abu El-Haj notes, the two terms are often used interchangeably.

However, there is another dimension to social justice that is not captured in the notion of equity. Connie North, who wrote a 2006 review of the concept of social justice, distinguishes between the "redistribution model of social justice" and the "recognition model of social justice."[17] The former focuses on correcting problems of unequal resources and unequal access to resources, while the latter focuses on changing cultural and institutional norms that misrecognize and devalue certain groups and individuals.

Let's look at an example that illustrates both of these models. In 1974, the landmark Supreme Court case *Lau v. Nichols* addressed complaints filed in lower courts in which Chinese speaking parents sued the San Francisco School District for not enabling their children to have equal access to instruction and curriculum. The school district first countered that they had provided the Chinese speaking children, who had limited or no English, with all the same materials, teachers, and other resources as the English speaking children. So what was the problem? They had provided "equality." However, the Supreme Court justices ended up ruling that by providing the English learners with the same materials, teachers, and instructional methods as the native English speaking children, the district had effectively denied the English learners the opportunity to learn. How could they learn the content, the justices argued, if they couldn't understand the textbooks or the teacher? The ruling in this case required school districts to seek and adopt ways to address this problem, whether through ESL classes, bilingual classes, or other specially designed instruction.

This case illustrates the difference between equality (providing the same resources to everyone) and equity (providing different resources to different children, depending on their background and needs, so that they can achieve the same educational outcomes). It also illustrates the notion of redistribution. Resources had to be distributed more equitably so that a group of learners would have equal access to learning opportunities.

But let's look at the same example in another way. In the court case, the valued commodity, if you will, is the ability to speak, read, and write English. The inability to speak English is treated as a problem that needs to be addressed. The ability to speak Chinese is not viewed as a positive attribute at all. What happens if we apply the recognition model here? It would mean that the school district (and individual teachers) would have to recognize Chinese language ability as a resource, alongside English speaking ability. This recognition might involve some practical changes, such as a class to teach Chinese to non-Chinese speakers, but above all it would be a cultural change in the way educators *value* those who speak other languages.

According to North, social justice is not a static concept. Its meanings change across times and spaces, but in her view, and ours, it should include both redistributive justice and recognition justice; it should aim to recognize and value both what we have in common and what differentiates us. And finally, it should take into account the way local issues of injustice are intertwined with global injustices.

Rosemary, one of the authors of this book, interviewed several education leaders about what equity and social justice mean to them. Edmundo Norte, the curriculum and professional development director for two charter schools, says,

> Inherent in those terms there's a critical view of society—a sense of inequity in the power structure....When I hear the term social justice, what it invokes is more of a lifestyle, an attitude and an orientation toward action, for how I operate in the world, what I do, the choices I make, what I support and don't support. It's how I try to live my life.

Hyon Chu Yi, who directs a multicultural center on a college campus, says,

> Because this is the work I do professionally, I can come up with a real technical definition, but I don't think of [social justice] as a law or technical definition. I think of it as a way of life.... It's the opportunity for everyone to pursue advancement in any field and that there aren't these barriers and restrictions that are institutionalized ... that prevent people from being full participants in our society.

Both Mr. Norte and Ms. Yi distance themselves from academic definitions, preferring to emphasize that equity and social justice are directly intertwined with their lives, personal as well as professional. For them, the commitment to the pursuit of a more just society enters every aspect of their lives; it cannot be "left at the office." Furthermore,

Mr. Norte points out that if there were no inequality, no injustice, we would not need to have these terms. The very existence of these terms in the English language implies that their opposites—inequity and social injustice—do exist.

So far, we have explained what we mean by "using language as a transformative force," and we have discussed the concepts of equity and social justice. The next question combines these two topics in asking "how"? What methods can we use to analyze language and bring it into our awareness more fully? This brings us to a discussion of critical discourse analysis and critical language awareness.

WHAT ARE CRITICAL DISCOURSE ANALYSIS AND CRITICAL LANGUAGE AWARENESS?

For reflection: If you were to analyze the language used in a conversation, or a meeting, or some other type of spoken discourse, how would you do it? What kinds of things would you pay attention to? What purposes would such an analysis serve?

Discourse, in the sense we are using it here, consists of "recurrent statements and wordings across texts" which "together mark out identifiable systems of meaning."[18] In other words, discourse is language *use* (as opposed to language as an abstract system or a set of prescriptive rules). To analyze discourse, we need to look at more than a sentence or two; usually, the texts that are analyzed consist of extended speech or writing—for example, a conversation, a meeting, an essay, an interview, or a political speech.

Discourse is always nested within some kind of a speech community whose members share certain background knowledge, which enables them to make sense of what is said. Some speech communities are very broad. For example, educational discourse in the United States contains identifiable wordings and patterns such as *dropouts*, *academic achievement*, and *college prep*—terms that are generally recognizable by most people in the United States, regardless of their educational background. But how many people in this vast group would know what an IEP is? Or how about the distinction between educational management and educational leadership? Smaller domains, such as special education and antiracist education, contain jargon that, while recognizable by insiders, is less accessible to outsiders. For insiders, these "buzzwords" carve out separate ideological spaces, whereas for outsiders, the buzzwords might be impenetrable or simply fail to connote the subtleties the insiders hear in them.

While some discourse analysts focus primarily on describing the structures of oral and written texts, others take what is known as a critical approach.[19] *Critical discourse analysis* is a research approach that seeks to establish connections between characteristics of texts (whether written, voiced, or signed), discourse practice (the way texts are produced, used, and distributed), and wider sociocultural practice (in other words, how texts fit into larger agendas, such as "globalization," "homeland security," etc.).[20] It is critical in the sense that it sets out to uncover connections between discourse and social practices that are generally not self-evident. It is especially concerned with uncovering unequal power relations and challenging the legitimacy of groups and institutions that oppress, marginalize, or silence people with less power. As such, it is often concerned with pointing out not only what people say or write and how they say or write it but also what (or who) they leave out. Omissions, in this type of analysis, become meaningful. For example, if an educational leader gives a welcome-back speech at the beginning of the school year and explicitly mentions students, parents, and teachers but does not mention the school staff members who work as custodians, secretaries, and cooks, one can reasonably question why these people are left out.

Critical language awareness shifts the focus from analysis and critique of discourses to "exploration and even advocacy of possible alternatives."[21] Critical language awareness is the application of critical discourse analysis as a force for change in actual domains of practice where unequal power relations are at issue.

Clearly, critical discourse analysis and critical language awareness are complementary aspects of one coherent effort. Taken together, the aim is to connect discourse at the micro level with its surrounding social context (macro level) and to use this analysis to argue for and implement changes in institutional practices. Simply put, critical discourse analysis may be described as the research part of this effort, and critical language awareness may be seen as the application of this research toward change in such domains as education, health care, the workplace, and politics.

Critical language awareness is still relatively unknown in preparation programs or inservices for teachers and school leaders. Most attempts to integrate critical language awareness in education focus on its development among students[22] rather than among educators. Where it does exist, the tendency is to focus on the relationships of power among different languages or varieties of language; for example, in the United States, the focus might be on the relationship between native speakers of English and native speakers of Spanish, African American Vernacular English, or Navajo. This attention to different languages and varieties of language is very important. But little attention has been given to *language as a medium for communication*—in other words, the way different wordings can convey different underlying beliefs.

In this book, we actively seek to make real the notion of critical language awareness as *awareness plus advocacy and action*. Some of the benefits we see are the following:

- Making visible assumptions that normally go unexamined
- Recognizing how language encodes social relations
- Identifying and challenging prejudice embedded in ordinary, daily discourse practices
- Interrogating and redirecting the nature of questions asked about schooling
- Raising questions that have not been asked

CONCLUSION AND SUMMARY OF KEY POINTS

As we've seen in the preceding sections, language can function as a transformative force in society, embodying not only critique of existing beliefs and practices, but also alternatives—a language of possibility. However, it's important to remember that language alone cannot create social change; to live up to its transformative potential, language change needs to be linked to other social actions, such as ensuring that all students have access to college preparatory classes or making sure our schools do not unwittingly assume that students of a certain ethnic group or economic class can only do "basic skills."

To understand *how* language shapes our beliefs and thinking, we briefly discussed the theoretical claims of Edward Sapir and Benjamin Whorf, linguists who argued that the first language we acquire as a child deeply affects the way we think. We also introduced George Lakoff's and Otto Santa Ana's work on metaphors, cognitive linguists who argue that metaphors are closely linked to the way our thinking is structured. Changing metaphors, they argue, can introduce a different perspective and interrupt assumptions that may be unhelpful. We then noted that schools and educational systems (in the United States and elsewhere) develop particular microcultures, including particular ways of using language that may promote assumptions about social hierarchy, separation of us and them, and so on.

Educators can use these theoretical notions about language as a tool in their quest to create more equitable schools and make social justice a reality. Using critical discourse analysis to uncover relations of power and inequality and applying critical language awareness as an everyday practice, we can begin to tap into the transformative power of language.

Cultivating and enacting language in these ways takes work. In the next chapter, we share some habits and strategies that educators find help them be more effective as change agents. Our journey is about to become more concrete as we dig more deeply into particular stories of how people have used language as a force for change.

NOTES

1. Fairclough, N. (2003). "Political correctness," p. 17.

2. Notwithstanding, individual African Americans sometimes prefer the older term, *Black*, in part because it is associated with the Black Power Movement.

3. Arriaza, G. and Arias, A. (1998). Claiming Collective Memory, pp. 70–79.

4. Although it is often referred to as the "Sapir-Whorf hypothesis," Sapir and Whorf did not actually frame their theoretical claim as a testable hypothesis. To read more about Sapir and Whorf's work and the relationship between language and thought, see Johnstone, B. (2008). *Discourse analysis*, pp. 36–43.

5. This is sometimes called *linguistic determinism*.

6. However, two things should be noted about the snow example. (1) Most of the Yup'ik Eskimo words for different kinds of snow are based on the same root form, with particles added onto the root to convey what type of snow it is. Yup'ik is called an *agglutinative* language, like German, in which you can add on many particles to a root and create very long words. Other languages like English tend to make these particles separate words (e.g., prepositions, adjectives). Therefore, the old adage that Eskimo languages have many more words for snow than English is based in part on a

misunderstanding of how different languages work. (2) If English speakers find themselves in a very cold, snowy environment for a period of time, they will rapidly develop all the necessary ways to distinguish among different types of snow—in English. We are very good at adapting our language to fit our environmental and social needs; there is nothing about English or any other language that makes it impossible to come up with lots of distinctions among types of snow. How those distinctions are expressed (e.g., by separate words or by phrases) will depend on the type of language it is.

7. Lakoff, G. (2004). *Don't think of an elephant,* p. xv.

8. By *frames* Lakoff means "mental structures that shape the way we see the world . . . they are part of what cognitive scientists call the 'cognitive unconscious'—structures in our brains that we cannot consciously access, but know by their consequences: the way we reason and what counts as common sense. We also know frames through language." Lakoff, G. (2004). *Don't think of an elephant,* p. xv.

9. Santa Ana, O. (2002). *Brown tide rising,* p. 298.

10. Varenne (1978) cited in Johnstone, B. (2008), *Discourse analysis,* p. 136.

11. A pseudonym.

12. Henze, R., Katz, A., Norte, E., Sather, S., and Walker, E. (1999). *Leading for diversity,* pp. 94–95.

13. For additional reading on critical pedagogy, see Friere (1970a, 1993), Guilherme (2002), and Wink (1997).

14. Santa Ana, O. (2002). *Brown tide rising,* p. 319.

15. In other words, by assuming that there is a certain level or standard which all students should achieve, this definition of equity does not question the inherent "rightness" or value of this standard. Abu El Haj, T. (2006). *Elusive justice,* p. 199.

16. Lindsay, R. Robins, K. and Terrell, R. (1999). *Cultural proficiency,* p. 79.

17. North, C. (2006). *More than words?* p. 508.

18. Luke, A. (1995). *Text and discourse in education,* p. 15.

19. For a good description of the differences between discourse analysis and critical discourse analysis, see Johnstone, B. (2008). *Discourse analysis,* pp. 27–29.

20. Fairclough, N. (1995). *Critical discourse analysis,* p. 87.

21. Fairclough, N. (1995). *Critical discourse analysis,* p. 221.

22. See for example Alim (2005) and Davis, Bazzi, Cho, Ishida, and Soria (2005).

CHAPTER TWO

Becoming Effective in Using Critical Language Awareness

Rethinking, proposing, and (re)formulating discourses is one thing, but having them accepted and adopted in the wider society is quite another. Traditions, ideologies, common sense, power, and interest may well be in the way.[1]

—Shi-Xu, *A Cultural Approach to Discourse*

As Shi-Xu, author of *A Cultural Approach to Discourse,* points out in the above quote, people who want to make changes in their schools or other institutions often have a hard time dealing with the various types of resistance they encounter. Being an effective change agent requires not only knowing *what* you want to change, but also *how*. This implies adopting habits that can help you communicate effectively with others.

We define *habit* as a disciplined thought process that has become so engrained in our daily behavior that we react without much thinking about what to do, like touch-typing. Once we have learned it, we can type any time, anywhere, even if we have stopped practicing it for a while. The habits we are referring to here include sets of understandings, skills, and strategies that aid our purposeful and continuous dismantling of oppressive language, as well as our ability to create alternatives that embody educational justice.

Some habits are quite specific and will be discussed in the later chapters. The ones we will discuss in this chapter are more general; they transcend specific situations.

Noticing How Language Constructs Our Social World

For reflection: Think of an experience when you suddenly started to notice something. What did you start to notice? What triggered your increased noticing?

We can probably all think of experiences in which we started to notice something more simply because we had recently learned something new about it, or had a conversation about it. While taking an art class, for example, Rosemary started to notice light and shadow more than she did before. The same phenomenon happens with language; the more we learn about it, the more we notice it in our everyday lives—we begin to hear details and notice patterns we didn't notice before. This noticing can happen in the form of self-monitoring, monitoring the language of others around us, and monitoring the language we see in written form. We are often amazed at what we notice as we begin to pay closer attention to language-in-use around us.

Several of the educators who participated in our studies said that once they began to notice language and its role in perpetuating inequities, they also experienced a phenomenon they called "catching [one]self." That is, the words would fly out of their mouths out of habit before they realized that those words did not match the beliefs they held. This catching phenomenon is very common, especially when people are undergoing some kind of shift of attitudes and behaviors. It can take some time for behaviors that we do automatically to be realigned with new or different beliefs. This is the difference between espoused theory and theory in practice—a notion we will discuss in more detail in Chapter 7. On the other hand, we have probably all seen and heard people who adopt politically correct language, without necessarily changing their underlying beliefs, attitudes, and actions.

To become more attuned to language in your everyday environment, it helps to keep the following questions in mind:

- *How are people classified?* When listening to people talk, ask yourself which people (individuals, groups) are represented in this stretch of talk? How are they represented? Is it by race? By gender? By socioeconomic status? By ethnicity? By primary language? By proficiency in English? By grade level? By immigration status? By sexual orientation? By religion?
- *What (or who) is being opposed or contrasted to what (or whom)?* Do you hear polar opposites like good/bad, strong/weak, smart/dumb, pass/fail, or legal/illegal? Which groups or individuals are characterized these ways? Is it systematic (e.g. are the smart kids always members of the same group)? What do these polarizing statements tell us about the way people around you are constructing differences? Which identities disappear in these polarizing characterizations?
- *Who or what is higher or lower in status?* In addition to polarizing, we often hear statements that imply hierarchies. Is one group depicted as better than or higher in status than another? Or are they presented as different but equal? What is it in the language that lets you know this? (This topic is the focus of Chapter 6.)
- *Who are the insiders and the outsiders?* Often in our everyday language, we cast some people as insiders and others as outsiders. For example, if we say, "As a reader of this book, you are already an educational leader," we assume that there are no readers of this book who do not already see themselves as educational leaders. Through this single statement, we have created an insider and an outsider group, and probably disenfranchised people who don't already consider themselves educational leaders.
- *What is the default case?* Usually whatever is considered normal or typical is not marked in language, whereas special cases and unusual situations are somehow marked or identified. For example, if a teacher says, "The Latino parents really value education," he has marked the parents who value education as a particular racial or cultural identity. He is implying that not all parents value education as much as the Latino parents. This default, or unmarked claim, is often

unspoken, but one can hear its presence as a shadowy contrast that gives meaning to the spoken statement about Latino parents. On the other hand, notice how the meaning changes if the speaker says, "**Those** Latino parents really value education" (with stress on "those"). This statement might convey to listeners the unmarked, or default, claim that most Latino parents do not value education. (For more on this phenomenon, see Chapter 3.)

- *What or who is left out?* In speaking as well as writing, we constantly select information to include or omit. Sometimes this selecting is done with our full awareness, but often it happens so quickly that we do not pause to think about what or whom we are leaving out.

- *What is being presumed?* In the statement, "Our school is really working hard to address the needs of the children," the speaker is assuming that the children have needs and that the school has correctly identified what those needs are. The emphasis is on the actions the school is taking to address those needs, not whether the needs themselves have been identified or whether reasonable people might disagree about what those needs are. In English, presumed information (or old information) can be signaled in various ways; one way is by using the definite article *the* plus a noun phrase. Another common way is by using a *when* clause. For example, in the sentence, "When Ms. Camejo was elected to the Board, she organized a parent advisory committee," the presumption is that Ms. Camejo was indeed elected to the Board.

RELATING THE TREES TO THE FOREST AND THE FOREST TO THE TREES

It's important to connect the patterns you see in language to broader social phenomena. A myopic focus on language without relating it to the larger context can end up being too narrow, and you will see only the trees but not the forest. So try to relate the micro to the macro and the macro to the micro. When you notice a pattern occurring in language (e.g., if you notice that certain people are regularly omitted from the discourse), ask yourself the following questions:

- What social relations or social process does this language reflect, reinforce, or reproduce?
- If I want to change these relations or process, what else besides language needs to change?
- How can I link language change with broader social change? Or the reverse—How can I link broader social change with ground-level changes that might be reflected in language?

IMAGINING ALTERNATIVES

When you read, hear, or use language that in some way perpetuates or reinforces social inequities, cultivate the habit of imagining alternatives:

- How could I (or you) have said this differently so that I (or you) would promote a more just situation?

This might involve actually revising what you said, suggesting an alternative to another person, silently imagining the alternatives without saying anything, or creating the space that invites others to imagine alternatives.

COACHING

For reflection: Have you ever had someone else "correct" your speech in a way that made you feel ashamed or angry? What was it about the way it was done that made you feel this way? Could it have been done in a way that you felt was all right or helpful?

Obviously, interrupting people's use of language in ways that shame or anger them will not help us accomplish our goals. In fact, we will just create inhibition or resistance and lose the opportunity to make a positive change in the culture around us. Effective coaching in critical language awareness helps people build greater awareness of the power of language. The coach must be very careful not to slide over into a policing role. Three key principles can guide us in effective coaching: Connecting before correcting, interrupting with grace, and thoughtful inaction.

Connecting Before Correcting[2]

Educational leaders who are effective coaches always try to build a relationship before they try to correct someone or suggest a different angle. Of course, it isn't always possible to have a well-developed relationship with everyone, especially if we work with multitudes of people. But the principle of "connect before you correct" is still an important one, regardless of how much time you have had to develop that connection. Even if a person is coming across as attacking or offensive, just acknowledging his or her feelings often helps. For example, "I imagine you must be feeling pretty frustrated right now because . . ." When people feel heard, they are more likely to be open to hearing what you have to say to them.

Interrupting With Grace

Another important element of coaching is doing it with grace, using strategies that preserve the dignity of the person you are coaching. The particular strategies you use will depend, of course, on your understanding of the person you are coaching—and that's why building a relationship of some kind is key in any type of coaching.

Several strategies are useful at this stage. They are seeking further explanation, interpreting, reframing, and paraphrasing:

- *Seeking further explanation* involves asking the speaker to clarify what is not obvious. For example, if someone you are coaching presents you with a classification of students as "ready for high school" and "need to be held back," you can ask, "Can you tell me what criteria you used to classify the students this way? Is there anyone who doesn't fit in these two categories?"
- *Interpreting* involves elucidating the unintended effects an utterance might have, or providing more context. For example, if someone you are coaching says, "Marisa really doesn't belong at this school; she's just a troublemaker," a possible interpretation could be, "You know, it's true that she's been involved in a lot of fights lately. But did you know that she was just moved to a group home after the last foster home she was in didn't work out? She's probably having an especially tough time right now adjusting to these changes."

- *Reframing* involves digging deeper to identify a speaker's underlying or most important issue, even if it is not the issue that is presented. For example, if the person you are coaching says, "I really don't see the need for all these meetings we're having about the students with low math skills," a possible reframing might be, "Is there something we should be doing that you think is missing in those meetings?"

- *Paraphrasing* (also sometimes called *reformulating*) involves restating an utterance in other words. Not only is this a good way to let the speaker know how his utterance might be understood; it also can be a good way to make sure you have understood. Common *stems*, or beginnings, are "let me see if I understood you correctly . . ." or "in other words, you are saying that . . ."

Thoughtful Inaction

In poker, a common saying is that you have to "know when to hold and know when to fold." In fact, in most realms of life, the importance of context in our decision making cannot be overstated. For educators who are practicing critical language awareness, acting on your new awareness doesn't always mean that you will immediately jump in and coach people. To do this could invite resistance and ridicule, and you will perhaps become known as the language police.

In certain contexts, you will have to decide whether it is wiser to interrupt or not. Often, these contexts will involve unequal power relations. Especially if you are in a subordinate position to the speaker you wish to interrupt, you will need to consider the risks involved. Your own job security might be at stake, or your positive relationship with this person. In some cases, age will be a factor. This concern may be particularly salient for those raised in cultures where younger people are expected to always obey (and not question or criticize) older people. Several of our interviewees also mentioned that it is difficult to interrupt family members because they will easily take offense and think you are being "uppity." In some cases, you may decide that it is more important to preserve those relationships than to enact your role as a change agent with them at that particular moment.

We emphasize the word *thoughtful* in front of inaction because we are suggesting that, while the context may make it a bad time to coach a person (or group) at that moment, this doesn't mean that you will simply drop the point altogether. (Here, the poker game metaphor falls apart, because as an educator your work is ongoing, not a series of separate card games.) Folding would mean giving up. Instead, our hope is that you would defer action, perhaps making a mental note of what was said so that you can bring it up at a later, more opportune time. Or if the power dynamics are such that you don't feel your status allows for effective intervention, you may want to refer the situation to a higher level of authority.[3]

TEACHING WITH CRITICAL LANGUAGE AWARENESS

For reflection: As a teacher, how do you deal with the fact that your curriculum is already heavily predetermined? Do you sometimes spontaneously slip in a lesson that was not part of your plan? What kinds of things do you slip in?

When you have opportunities, either in the classes you teach or in workshops or institutes or other situations in which you are the facilitator, try to integrate with your work a focus on critical language awareness. One of the best strategies for doing this is to *link* it to something you already do.

Linking Critical Language Awareness to Other Topics

Maybe you already teach something that is related, for example, something about being a change agent, or something about the use of different languages in educational settings. We have found that when language is addressed in educational settings, the focus is usually on the use of different languages (e.g., English, Spanish, Farsi) and bilingualism and bilingual education or on hate language and slurs (i.e., the *N*-word). You can link critical language awareness to the above topics in the following ways:

- *If you are teaching about being a change agent,* one way to actively pursue your role is to be critical of the language you use and help other people find alternatives that will more clearly support your shared vision and goals. Ask your students: What language do we need to change to be consistent with our goals for social (or environmental) change?

- *If you are teaching about the use of different languages in educational settings,* often the underlying issue is about creating spaces for people to affirm and practice their cultures. This may also come up with regard to different dialects and other varieties of language (e.g., occupational jargon, slang). You can connect these topics to critical language awareness by pointing out that whether we all speak the same language or different ones, we have choices about whether we use language to exclude people or include them, whether to classify them this way or another way, and so on.

- *If you are teaching about the use of hate language and slurs,* you are probably focusing on what *not* to say; in other words, the focus is on avoiding what is harmful or negative. A good link to critical language awareness can be made by adding a positive twist: We not only want to focus on what *not* to say but also on *imagining alternatives.* What can we say that can support us achieving a more just and equitable society?

USING MEMORABLE EXAMPLES, METAPHORS, AND QUOTES

The educators we interviewed and observed use concrete examples, metaphors, and pithy, memorable quotes to help them communicate about social justice, equity, and the power of language. Here are a few of the quotes they shared with us:

- "The master's tools will never dismantle the master's house" (Audre Lorde).[4]
- "No problem can be solved by the same consciousness that created it" (Einstein).[5]
- "Washing one's hands of the conflict between the powerful and the powerless means to side with the powerful, not to be neutral" (Paolo Friere).[6]
- "People see things as they are and ask why; others dream things that never were and ask, why not?" (George Bernard Shaw).[7]

But lest we imply that it is only famous people who say memorable things, we also want to point out that later in this book, you will come across excellent "quotable quotes" by the people who have participated in our studies.

Many quotes contain good content, so what is it about a really memorable quote that makes it "stick" in people's minds? Edmundo Norte says he is drawn to quotes that "tell us something about our potential"; in other words, they "foster ongoing personal transformation" in some way. Quotes that tap into our emotions also seem to help—"the heart connection before the head connection" as Mr. Norte puts it, and illustrates with another quote: "In every human heart, there is a longing for certainty and repose; but certainty is generally an illusion and repose is not the destiny of human kind" (Oliver Wendell Holmes).[8]

MODELING TEAMWORK, INCLUSIVENESS, AND RESPECT

Another way to offer or present a language of possibility is by modeling group processes that are appropriate to the goals of social justice and equity. To see how this and other habits are materialized in real situations, we now turn to a snapshot from one of the leaders who participated in Rosemary's study.

A Vignette of a Professional Development Day

It is August, 2007, and school is going to begin in a couple of weeks. The teachers and administrators of two charter high schools in the Bay Area are gathered together for Day 1 of a weeklong series of staff development days. The facilitator, Mr. Norte, whom we introduced earlier, works for two charter schools, both of which are operated by the same nonprofit organization. He begins the day with two activities: In the first one, he asks participants to sit in groups and discuss their greatest hopes for this staff development series. After they have discussed these hopes in small groups, he asks each group to share with the whole group while he writes their contributions on the board. In the next activity, he uses the same procedure but this time asks people to focus on their greatest concerns.

Throughout the day, Mr. Norte uses language that highlights teamwork, inclusivity, and respect. He uses questions such as "How can we support each other to . . . ?" and "How can we maximize our potential?" Often, before writing something on the board, he reformulates their statements or phrases as questions. For example, when one participant said, "Students aren't aware of the graduation requirements," Mr. Norte reformulated the statement as "How do we make sure students are aware of the graduation requirements?" However, when putting a reformulated statement or question on the board, he checks in with the individual, asking "Does this work?" or "Does this capture it?"

These questions help move the group more in the direction of joint actions because questions inevitably position the listener as a potential respondent. Instead of only hearing a concern, the teachers begin to try to answer the question; they are already beginning to think about how to solve the problem.

The other point about these questions is that Mr. Norte almost always uses *we*. If he used a different pronoun or noun in place of *we*, the effect would be completely different. *You*, for example, would mean he didn't include himself. *One* is ambiguous and vague; it could be anybody—or nobody! And identifying a specific person or group would mean others could separate themselves and not feel any responsibility. In other words, there would be no joint action, no joint problem solving. Of course, later on in the session, the group does assign specific individuals to take the lead on certain tasks. Obviously, it isn't practical for everyone to be equally involved in everything that goes on in a school. But for a staff development session on its first day, preparing for the year ahead, looking at the big picture, and trying to build a sense of community, the *we* is totally appropriate.

Mr. Norte consistently uses *Mr.* and *Ms.* as titles in the staff development session. About this choice, he says,

There's a term that I heard a long time ago, it's called "lifestyle activism." Whatever you do, in every moment . . . it's like integrity, how you're talking to a clerk at the checkout stand, how you're talking to the cop that stops you, how you talk to your kids, your family members, a stranger on the street, the person who busses your dishes at a restaurant . . . there's ways that you can resist [the status quo stratification our society imposes on us], like saying señor, señora, speaking with respect, recognizing them. . . . I'm going to reinforce that you're a whole human being who's worthy of dignity and respect, so it's like, reinforcing that in every little moment that we have a chance.

A good coach doesn't focus on telling others what to do or not do. Effective coaching involves demonstrating the habits that you hope others will try. Mr. Norte modeled teamwork and inclusiveness when he consistently framed future actions to be done by *we* rather than *you* or *they.* He also organized the activities of the day in a way that encouraged participants to take ownership over identifying concerns *and* identifying solutions. He practiced "reformulating" when he changed statements of concern into written questions so as to stimulate a search for answers, the beginning of problem solving. He also practiced respect when, instead of simply appropriating or reframing a statement, he checked in with participants about whether the reformulation captured it.

One other point that Mr. Norte made later on, during an interview, is that when he practices these habits such as teamwork, inclusion, and others, he usually calls people's attention to the habit or practice itself, often at the end of an activity. He might say, for example, "What we just did is a technique called *think-pair-share.* Did you notice how everybody in the room got a chance to participate more? This is something you can adapt and use with your students." This last habit might be called *increasing metacognitive awareness*, and it is important because when we model something, we cannot assume that everybody will pick up on what we intended to model. Being explicit about it can be very helpful because it gives people a frame for these types of experiences.

Each of these habits by itself might not amount to much. But taken as a whole, they demonstrate integrity of purpose. Mr. Norte is a good example of an educational leader who really tries to "walk the talk" as well as "talk the talk."

ACTIVITY: OBSERVING AN EDUCATOR

Think of an educator you know who you think embodies the positive language habits we have discussed in this chapter. Next time you see this person, observe closely how he or she uses language, as well as how the people around respond. (Keep a notepad handy to jot down some of the things this person and others say.) Afterwards, analyze your notes to see which of the habits discussed in this chapter were used. Were there any other strategies that we didn't mention? Would you make any improvements if you were in this situation?

CONCLUSION AND SUMMARY OF KEY POINTS

To effectively practice critical language awareness in an institutional context such as a school, it helps to develop certain habits that enable you to work with people in a positive way.

These include (1) paying attention to the way language constructs our social world (e.g., are there insiders and outsiders?); (2) connecting the big picture to the details (e.g., is there a connection between the way people talk and the larger social reality?); (3) imagining how we could use language in ways that would be more reflective of the social reality we desire to see; (4) coaching other people in a way that preserves their dignity and allows them to take in what you are trying to say; (5) infusing critical language awareness in your teaching; (6) using memorable examples, metaphors, and quotes to help you communicate clearly and vividly; and (7) modeling teamwork, inclusiveness, and respect in all the work we do—in other words, we need to "walk the talk"!

NOTES

1. Shi-Xu (2005). *A cultural approach to discourse*, p. 97.
2. Thanks to Edmundo Norte for this phrasing.
3. The following youtube link, "The power of one voice" has footage of some model interactions in which people speak out to interrupt oppressive behavior: http://www.youtube.com/watch?v=WIT8I04JYIk.
4. Lorde, A. (1984). *Sister Outsider*, p. 110.
5. Albert Einstein.
6. Friere, P. (1970b). Cultural action and conscientization.
7. Shaw, G. B. (1921).
8. Holmes, O. (1897/2004). *The path of law*, p. 10.

CHAPTER THREE

Avoiding Othering: Practicing Including

INTRODUCTION

> A student in my multicultural literature class made the statement that women who cover themselves from head to toe in Muslim countries are extremist. So I told him that we have to be careful about how we use words like *extreme*, especially when we are referring to different groups of people, and that the word *extremist*, when used with people of the Middle East, particularly, can have a very negative connotation. Then a Muslim student in the class explained about Muslim women and some of the reasons for dressing as they do. Other students had things to say. It was a really good discussion. The discussion ended, though, with a student saying that the word *extremist* is just a word and it doesn't mean anything. (Dorothy Allen, a high school teacher)

We begin with this example because it illustrates rather well the dynamics of othering. A high school student uses the word *extremist* to describe Muslim women who cover their entire bodies. So what? It is a seemingly unobjectionable use of language—and yet, the teacher, Ms. Allen, reacted to it and spent some class time "unpacking" the term, pointing out that it might have negative connotations. Why did she take the time? What is it about this term, in this context, that makes it problematic?

Othering is a way of using language to make other people different from *me* or *us*. When done in a context in which *I* or *we* are part of the dominant group or the ones in power and the other people are part of a minority or less powerful group, othering usually has the effect of making *I*, or the *we* group seem "normal" and the others "strange." The term *extremist* in the above example would have no meaning if it were not implicitly contrasted with those who are not extreme (i.e., "normal"). Without actually saying so, this student is conveying to the listeners the idea that he himself is normal.

The concept of *other* originated in the writing of Hegel, the 19th century German philosopher, and later appeared in the writings of Lacan, a 20th century French philosopher and psychiatrist. In its original use, the "other" refers to a child's recognition of him- or herself as a distinct entity, separate from the rest of the world. Psychoanalysts write of a "mirror stage" in which a child first acquires this recognition. Scholars such as Simone de Beauvoir, who wrote *The Second Sex* (1949), and Edward Said, author of the 1978 book *Orientalism,* later took the concept and applied it to situations involving the dominance and subordination of whole groups. Feminist and other contemporary scholars now frequently use the concept of othering in their writing. It appears in the educational literature as well, especially in the work of those who take a critical approach.[1]

Scholars take different positions on whether othering is always negative or harmful. Some point out that it is a necessary aspect of identity formation—that we have to create the other as a kind of foil to identify what we are not; these categories and contrasts help us develop a sense of who we are in relation to others.[2] This kind of othering, minus any harmful effect, might be called "friendly othering."

Felecia Briscoe, one of this book's authors, argued in her 2005 article that othering is also more complex than we might initially think: "The other is not just a boundary we cross from time to time; the other is always within us."[3] This is because we are constantly juggling various identities (e.g., our roles within our families, our professions, our gender, our ethnicity, our racial identity, our sexual orientation). The identity that comes forward as salient in a given situation may be one that we choose to highlight—or it may be selected for us by our social positioning in that context. We don't always have control over how others see us.

For the purposes of this book, we will be using the term *othering* in the sense it was used by Edward Said: that is, to signify a discourse process in which a dominant or more powerful group or individual distances itself from a subordinate or less powerful group or individual.

A CHANGE AGENT IN ACTION

Ms. Allen, whom we quoted at the beginning of this chapter, has played a pivotal role in creating changes at the large, urban high school in Northern California where she teaches. Beginning early in her career there in the 1970s, she advocated for systematic attention in the curriculum to students' identities as African Americans, Latinos, Native Americans, Asian Americans, and European Americans. As she says, "We would be on the road to unity—if everybody felt like they belonged." In other words, if a school wants to create a sense of unity among all the stakeholders in the school (e.g., students, parents, faculty, staff), the school needs to actively create a sense of belonging for every individual and for every group.

Although it took a long time, her efforts and those of other teachers eventually bore fruit in terms of lasting institutional changes. Now, her school district is one of the few in the United States that has a multicultural studies requirement for high school graduation. Students must complete a semester's worth of study, choosing from a menu of courses offered by the Ethnic Studies Department (also a new development, thanks to Ms. Allen's and other people's efforts). They can choose a course that deals specifically with one ethnoracial group, such as Filipino American Heritage or African American History, or they can select a more general course such as Issues in Ethnic Studies.[4] Not only have her efforts to make the school more inclusive of all students profoundly affected the institution as a whole and the group of teachers whom she has mentored, but she also practices critical language awareness inside the classroom with her own students.

Ms. Allen, who is African American, regularly teaches the African American History and African American Issues classes in which, as one student put it, "We study what has been left out of the regular history books." She also teaches required courses in U.S. History. Many African American students take the courses that deal with African American History and Issues but so do students of other ethnic groups. Ms. Allen is a very popular teacher. Having observed several of her classes, Rosemary, one of this book's authors, noted how students of different ethnic backgrounds learned from each other—African American, African, Middle Eastern, and European Americans frequently challenged each other in class to rethink common assumptions about what it means to be *black*, *white*, *brown*, or *mixed*. In Ms. Allen's classes, it is common to see taken-for-granted categories unearthed and examined from multiple perspectives.

Keeping in mind this snapshot of Ms. Allen's role as a change agent, let's return to the example of the student who described Muslim women who cover themselves from head to toe as *extremists*. The question of "so what?" remains. So what if we use othering expressions in our everyday language? It doesn't hurt anybody—or does it?

How Is Othering Harmful?

In this section, we want to emphasize two ways in which othering can be harmful. One way is by harming the person or group who is othered. The second way is by ignoring the complexity of the person who does the othering.

Distancing and Deriding the "Other"

Why did Ms. Allen question the student's use of the word *extremist*? She thought it had a negative connotation, especially when used to describe Muslim women in today's post-9/11 context. This word has been used in the media and in political speeches to describe individuals conspiring to cause us harm. So the student probably inadvertently made the connection between religious fundamentalism and terrorism, perhaps not realizing that many women in Afghanistan and Iran wear the *burka* (full covering) because they have to, not necessarily because they want to. And even if they choose to wear it, this does not make them terrorists. Similarly, it would be unwise to assume that anyone in the United States with a Latino surname is an undocumented immigrant.

One of the key effects of othering is that we use language to cast people who are different from ourselves as not only different but also weird, strange, extreme, incomprehensible, mysterious, inscrutable, violent, and so on. Part of the harm, especially when this is done in public spaces, is that we are asserting negative or abnormal attributes to people we don't really know; we end up stereotyping people, lumping them all together as a big group with no distinctions or individual variation. People in subordinate positions often internalize these stereotypes about themselves; they may come to see themselves as fitting that stereotype, especially if they are children, who are vulnerable because they don't yet have the critical consciousness to resist stereotypes about themselves.

As a side note, it may be helpful here to make some distinctions among terms. According to linguist Teun Van Dijk, *stereotyping* is a perceptual matter; we perceive what we don't understand well as a generalized mass. Stereotypes can of course be reflected in our discourse, through expressions like "women are nurturing" or "Muslim women who wear the *burka* are extremists." But is stereotyping necessarily the same as othering? Not exactly.

Othering is a linguistic process that often *draws on* common stereotypes of people forced into subordination. In other words, stereotypes are perceptions, and stereotyping is a process of making generalizations about a group. Othering is a broader process than stereotyping because it includes not only stereotyping the other but also simply distancing oneself—for example, referring to the other as *they* or *those people*. It also includes communicating that the other is not like us.

Marginalizing and *excluding* are also closely related to othering. The main point to keep in mind is that othering is a linguistic process realized through discourse (either oral, signed, or written), whereas marginalizing and excluding are social phenomena. For example, the use of othering in discourse may serve to reflect, reinforce, or construct a group's marginal status in society, but that marginal status is probably related as well to job discrimination, inferior schooling, and so on. In other words, the linguistic process of othering is only *partially* responsible for marginalizing and excluding people. Other social and institutional actions are involved as well.[5]

Here is another example that Ms. Allen recounted:

> We were having a discussion in U.S. History and one student realized that an African American student who just moved to [the Bay Area] from Louisiana was not in class. Instead of referring to him by his name, she asked, "Where's the guy who talked funny?" The class knew who she was talking about and so did I. I asked her what she meant by *funny*. She responded by saying "the guy who talks different." At that point I asked her if she was referring to LeShawn, the student from Louisiana, and she said yes. I said that it was his southern accent that made him sound different, and if we were in the South, Southerners would say that we talked funny or different because of our California accents. Other students chimed in about folks with accents from other parts of the United States and what they say about California accents. Finally, I asked if she still

wanted to say that LeShawn had a funny or different accent. She said no and that from now on she would say that LeShawn had a unique accent. Then we went on with history. I thought that it was a pretty fruitful lesson.

All speakers have accents. An *accent* is just the particular realization of three elements: (1) consonant and vowel sounds, (2) intonation (the "melody" of our speech with all its ups and downs), and (3) voice quality (we recognize a friend's voice on the phone almost immediately by its voice quality—whether it is nasal, breathy, etc.). Likewise, people who sign also have their own accents depending on where they learned to sign. When we hear someone insisting that he or she doesn't have an accent, what is really going on? Could it be that this person has *no* distinguishing features in his or her speech?[6]

The perception of accent is relative. If you have lived in New York City all your life, and interacted mostly with other New Yorkers, you are going to sound like them, bearing in mind that even in New York City, many variations on a New York accent exist. Because you are surrounded by people who sound similar to you, you might not think of yourself as having a noticeable accent—until you travel elsewhere and the people you encounter make fun of your accent!

As in the earlier example about Muslims from Ms. Allen's class, the student who talked about LeShawn's "funny accent" was positioning herself as normal—not having a funny accent. What she was really saying was that she fits in and LeShawn doesn't. He is an outsider, from somewhere else. Probably other things mark him as an outsider as well—perhaps his values or beliefs differ from those of the majority of students in the school, or perhaps his name is unusual. But values and beliefs, because they are more abstract, are less likely to be the immediate target of othering. Accent, like skin pigmentation, hair, personal names, and clothing, is a readily available, concrete marker that one can point to as a sign of difference.

The student's alternative to "funny accent" in this scenario is "unique accent." *Unique* seems to encode the idea that we perceive accents differently depending on where we are and who is in the majority. While it may be a trivial attempt by a student to get the teacher off her back, it also suggests that some learning may have taken place. In any case, "unique accent" suggests something of value rather than something to be derided, and it presupposes that we all have accents. This would be an example of friendly othering rather than othering as deviancy.

This particular example may seem pretty innocuous—but it doesn't take much to imagine how it could become harmful. Accents, especially foreign-language accents, are regularly used as a tool of derision and mockery on schoolyards across the United States. Students from Asian countries are said to talk "chinkytalk" and those doing the mocking will actually "imitate" the sounds they imagine. The message is always the same—you don't belong. You are an outsider, a foreigner, an "other." The people doing the mimicry are members of the more dominant group in that situation, and they have the power to deride the less powerful by highlighting their "otherness," their difference from the "norm."

Ms. Allen has commented many times that it's much easier to get young people to change their behavior than adults. "With the students, it takes a minute; they get it." And she says her students will "spread" what they learned in her classes to other teachers' classes too. This is evidence that they have "bought into" what they learned. With adult colleagues, however, she feels it's much harder to influence behavior "because we're always intellectualizing, trying to appear smarter."

Blinding the Powerful

The second layer of harm involved in othering is much more subtle. This is the implicit assumption that the speaker (and those who, like the speaker, are in a position of power) does *not* have those features the speaker considers deviant or negative. *We* are normal, and we take our own normalcy for granted. It is not even open for questioning.

But why, one might wonder, is this assumed normalcy harmful? The main reason is that it allows people who are part of the dominant culture to maintain a certain blindness about their own positions, practices, beliefs, and attitudes. It functions as a kind of cultural amnesia.

Rosemary recalls a conversation she had with Gail,[7] a European American woman who had spent several years teaching and doing research in Hawai'i. Rosemary had recently returned to California after six months as a visiting professor at the University of Hawai'i. As they discussed their experiences, the topic turned to the Hawaiian language renewal movement. Gail at one point said, "They [Native Hawaiian language activists] would make a lot more progress if only they didn't have so much conflict within the group." This is an othering statement in that Gail was implying that native Hawaiian people should behave as a monolithic group, and simultaneously that the dominant group (unstated, but possibly white people or people like herself) makes progress because it has no such internal conflict.

Rosemary remembers responding along these lines: "But don't we have conflicts too? Just because they are Native Hawaiians doesn't mean they should all act the same way and have the same agendas." Gail laughed and agreed.

At the community level, we can see the dynamics of othering taking place when longtime residents feel threatened or challenged by newcomers. A sad case in point appeared in an article called "Our town," by Alex Kotlowitz.[8] Carpenterville, a small town outside of Chicago, has recently been experiencing rapid growth in the number of Latino immigrants. "An estimated 40% of its 37,000 residents are Hispanic, a jump from 17% in 1990." A group calling themselves "the All American Team," led by two longtime residents, formed to seek election to the town's board. Their platform was to "do everything in their power to discourage illegal immigrants from settling in Carpenterville." While ostensibly aimed only at those without documentation, their campaign unleashed a chain reaction with clearly racist repercussions. On the day before the election, a flier was sent to two thousand families in town. Among other things, it said,

> Are you tired of seeing multiple families in our homes? Are you tired of not being able to use Carpenter Park on the weekend because it is overrun by Illegal Aliens? [sic] Are you tired of reading that another Illegal alien was arrested for drug dealing? . . . If you are as tired as me then let's get out and Vote for the: All American Team. . . . Finally, a team that will help us take back our town! (Kotlowitz, p. 36)

In addition to European Americans and recent arrivals from Latin America, many of the town's residents are U.S. citizens of Mexican or Latino American ancestry. Many have a foothold in the middle class. The rhetoric of the All American Team offended them deeply because it felt "less like a debate on illegal immigration than it did a condemnation of Hispanic culture" (Kotlowitz, p. 37). At the heart of this debate is the question of who is "American." In Carpenterville, the debate was framed as a conflict between Anglo-American longtime residents and "the other"—in this case, all people of Latino background.

While the harmful effects of this campaign will be felt for a long time to come by local Latinos, both with and without papers, another party is harmed as well—the seemingly privileged, empowered group who led the campaign. They implied a very narrow definition of *American* that doesn't take into account our long history as a country of immigrants. If one group is currently targeted as the "other," what does that mean for the rest of us? Will Japanese Americans be the next target, as they were in World War II? Or how about Italian Americans? Is anyone really safe? Who has the right to be called an American? And when it is used so exclusively, doesn't this undermine our constitution, which guarantees freedom and justice for all?

This effort to address some of the problems the town was experiencing could have been handled very differently. For instance, leaders in the European American community and the Latino community and business owners could have organized a task force to research and identify the most pressing problems and engage the rest of the community in developing solutions. If undocumented workers were indeed part of the problem, then questions would need to be asked about why they are in Carpenterville. Obviously, they fill a need for workers that isn't met with the existing workforce. Why? Are wages so depressed that citizens and permanent residents won't take those jobs?

Language matters. Rather than casting the problem in *us* versus *them* terms, it could have been framed differently. Rather than using the words *All American Team* (which implicitly constructs some people as NOT *all American,* the concerned citizens could have chosen a banner that would unite people of all sectors—for example, the *Unity Team* or the *Solutions Together Team*. Of course, a different name does not erase the underlying attitudes that led to the "All American Team" in the first place. For real change to occur, we cannot simply use politically correct language and assume that does the trick. Nonetheless, changing language is part of the larger change process—necessary, but not sufficient.

To take another example, recently, China has been under a lot of scrutiny for its human rights abuses. When U.S. leaders talk about China's sullied record, they never mention that the United States has some human rights issues of its own—why do the majority of Latinos, African Americans, Native Americans, and poor students of all ethnic backgrounds still receive an inferior education in this country? Isn't equal educational opportunity supposed to be a right of all children in this country?

Why were the victims who suffered the most in Hurricane Katrina African American? It was a "natural" disaster, yes, but was it "natural" that the vast majority of people stuck in overcrowded shelters with inadequate food, water, and sanitation were African American? Why do millions of U.S. citizens have no health care?

The implicit assumption is that the United States is clean and clear of such abuses, but a little questioning of these assumptions leads us to some pretty grievous human rights issues of our own. Othering masks domestic issues that need attention. By making *them* look bad, we make *us* look good—or at least passing. Likewise, when educational leaders talk about the bad parenting of *those* minority group parents, without mentioning the bad parenting found in all groups, they implicitly give the majority group parents a pass.

The very fact that this assumed normalcy is implicit rather than overt makes it more insidious. When messages of racism and prejudice are overt and blatant, listeners may be less easily influenced by them because the norms against racism predispose people to resist these kinds of messages. The more subtle and indirect expressions involved in othering may therefore be more effective in influencing people to uncritically accept the underlying messages.[9]

While recognizing and critiquing othering when it occurs is an important step in the right direction, it is not enough. One of Ms. Allen's colleagues puts it succinctly: "What's the use of training a bunch of cynics?" We can critique language all we want, but this in itself does not provide a direction for change. We all need to think of alternatives, ways of using language that are more inclusive and less likely to create rigid boundaries between *us* and *them*.

DIGGING DEEPER INTO OTHERING

We have discussed why othering has the potential to be harmful. Next, we turn to some key elements that will help clarify how othering can be recognized and addressed.

Marked and Unmarked Identities

To understand the way othering works, it helps to understand what is happening linguistically.

Othering depends on a basic distinction we have available to us—all languages are capable of marking utterances, or not marking them. In linguistics, *markedness* refers to the way words are changed or added to give a special meaning. The *unmarked choice* is just the ordinary meaning . . . If I meet you and say "Hi, how are you?" you may or may not even answer the question. But if I say "Hi, how's your dad?" this is special. You are likely to think of the question as actually asking how your dad is.[10]

To put it simply, *marking* is indicating that something is special or deviant from the norm and highlighting that specialness linguistically. For example, *tiger* is the unmarked word, whereas *tigress* is marked for *female*. When we make a person or a group into an "other," we usually rely on the linguistic device of marking to point out that we are referring to an unusual situation, not the everyday, taken-for-granted situation.

Take for example, the following statements about a position at Deere Tractors in the United States. Which of these statements is the *least marked* statement?

1. An Asian man applied for the CEO[11] position.

2. A woman applied for the CEO position.

3. A man applied for the CEO position.

4. Someone applied for the CEO position.

Most people would select number four. It doesn't give any explicit clues as to who applied, so we are left to fall back on our culturally-shaped assumptions and assume it was probably a European American man. Traditionally, tractors are driven by men, and knowing about mechanical things is a male domain. We also tend to assume that, unless otherwise indicated, a CEO in the United States is most likely to be a European American male.

Number three is a little odd, given the previous explanation. If the normal thing is for men to apply, why should it even be mentioned that the applicant was a man? Maybe the majority of applicants up to now have been women? Or maybe this is not a CEO of Deere Tractors, but a CEO of a subdivision of Deere Tractors that is trying to attract women to buy tractors? Numbers one and two are clearly marked; number two indicates that it was a woman (not a man, as might be expected) who applied, and number one indicates that the man who applied was not European American, as might be expected, but Asian.

Here's another example: In a music playgroup for toddlers in an upper-middle-class neighborhood in the San Francisco Bay Area, European American biological mothers were the unmarked identity among caregivers. Fathers, who were present in smaller numbers, were considered unusual, as were grandparents and nonrelated nannies. Each of these unusual identities was marked linguistically through the types of comments and questions participants addressed to caregivers who did not fit the norm, as the examples that follow show. European American mothers, on the other hand, were given no special explanations or descriptions.

Without being aware of it, we tend to linguistically mark those we consider unusual participants in a particular setting. So when fathers showed up at the playgroup, they often heard things like this: "Oh, are you Johnny's dad? It's great that you could come." Such comments would not be directed to Johnny's mother. When we talk about a particular community, usually one type of identity is "unmarked." It is constructed as the default condition, not needing any special explanation or notice.[12]

How to Recognize Marking

As you might expect, the languages of the world offer a multitude of ways to accomplish othering. Although we focus here on English, readers who speak other languages can probably think of many ways in which this is done in different languages. Below are a few of the ways to mark otherness in English:

- Special endings: *ette* or *ess* to designate a female form (e.g., *tiger*, *tigress*)
- Adjectives: a *strange* language as opposed to a language
- Nouns that act as modifiers: welfare mothers as opposed to mothers
- Pronouns signifying distance versus proximity: *those* kids as opposed to *these* kids; *they/them* versus *we/us*. (e.g., I wonder why *they* are always fighting?—The assumption is that *we* do not always fight.)
- Stress on the marked item: They gave the job to a *man*! (as opposed to a woman)

- Reported speech or quoted speech: these forms tend to distance the speaker from the voice of the other. (e.g., *It was alleged* that the teacher made a racist comment in class.)
- Negative constructions such as: *You don't understand us,* or *You can't work with the kids in this community because you're not one of us.*

Rosemary teaches in a master's degree program that prepares people to be teachers of English as a second language. About half of her students are local, having grown up somewhere in the South Bay, near San José. Another half is international students who are planning to go back and teach English in their home countries. In the field known as TESOL (Teaching English to Speakers of Other Languages), there has been an upsurge lately in scholarly discussions and debates about the relative advantages of being a native speaker of the language you teach, versus being a non-native speaker.[13]

The default or assumed normal situation is for a language teacher to be a native speaker of the language she or he is teaching. For many years, it was also assumed that these native-speaking teachers had a natural advantage over non-native-speaking teachers (who, by the way, have been constructed as *other* by the usage of *non*, which implies that native English-speaking teachers are the norm). This assumption is played out worldwide in thousands of job ads for English language teachers, in which "native speakers only" are invited to apply. And even when the job ads do not say so explicitly, the interviewers usually favor native speakers, even when they don't have as much experience or preparation as non-native-speaking applicants.

To be sure, native speakers do have a good intuitive grasp of the language as well as the cultural norms of the English-speaking communities where they have lived. But does that necessarily make them good *teachers* of the language? Recent research has begun to question the old assumptions, finding many areas in which non-native-speaking teachers actually might be better teachers, or as good as native-speaking teachers. For instance, a well-prepared, non-native-speaking teacher has spent many years learning English and therefore has first hand experience with the process of learning it. This often gives the non-native-speaking teacher a great deal of empathy for the difficulties students will encounter as they struggle to learn it.

Furthermore, non-native-speaking English teachers usually are more keenly aware of the grammar of English—again, because they had to learn it themselves, whereas native English-speaking teachers, even when well prepared, often find themselves unable to explain grammatical patterns. They know what "sounds right" to their ears, but they may be at a loss to provide a student with a clear explanation. How many native English speakers can easily explain, for example, why we say "call off the meeting" or "call the meeting off" or "call it off," but we cannot say "call off it"?[14]

There is a further problem with the native/non-native construct. Not only does it immediately cast non-natives as the other, but it also constructs a polarized and oversimplified world in which all English teachers have to fit into one of these two mutually exclusive categories. You can probably think of people who don't fit these categories, or who complicate the binary distinction. Rosemary finds many in her graduate classes—students who grew up in the United States in bilingual homes, for example, who consider themselves native speakers of both Spanish and English. Or people who have grown up in India, or Singapore, or Kenya, where English is one of the national languages. They speak English natively but what they speak is not United States English or British English but the local variety of English in their country.

The point we are making is that this simple construction—native-English-speaking teacher and non-native-English-speaking teacher—casts the non-native as the other, and reinforces a reductive, overly simplistic way of thinking about the world. In fact, this oversimplification causes bilinguals and people who grew up in places such as India or Singapore to simply "disappear" from the categorization system—a topic we will take up in more depth in Chapter 7.

FROM OTHERING TO INCLUSION AND DIALOGUE

How can we provide an alternative way of framing in the above situation involving native and non-native teachers of English? There is no formula, but here is one alternative: Advertisements that seek English-language teachers should be written in such a way that they focus on the actual skills and preparation the employer desires, rather than focusing on the false binary of native/non-native. For instance, if the employers want someone with excellent skills in teaching grammar and writing in a U.S. academic context, the advertisement should clearly state the skills that are desired. Second, it should try to reverse the default expectation by stating explicitly that bilinguals as well as native speakers are invited to apply.

We have already seen some other reframing examples:

- The student with the "funny accent" was reframed as a person with a "unique accent." This transformed the original negative othering into a friendly othering.
- Instead of calling the leadership group in Carpenterville the "All American Team," it could be renamed "Solutions Together" or "Unity Team."

Reframing skills can be built by using language opposite to othering—that is, striving to be inclusive in our language; explicitly recognizing and valuing different perspectives; acknowledging the complexity of the dominant (speakers') group. These are all examples of practicing a "language of possibility." Activities 4 and 5 provide some concrete practice in applying these skills.

ACTIVITIES

In this section, we suggest a few activities that will provide practice in recognizing othering, analyzing it, and considering various alternatives or reframings that offer a "language of possibility."

Activity 1: Analyzing an Excerpt

Following are two excerpts from interviews. Create your own discussion questions about them, and/or discuss those that are given.

I hear among teachers "those kids," and I know they mean the poor, ELDs, Latinos. (Lupe,[15] a school administrator)

"Those kids" always refers to kids with discipline issues. I feel they're [teachers are] blaming kids for their own inability to connect with kids. It's not their fault—the teachers' lack of understanding the socioeconomic, learning challenges, etc. that "those kids" confront—but the student's fault. They become angry to these kids for having problems. They assume kids should have the skills already, and because they don't, they get angry at them. How can you know something you've never lived or taken the time to learn about? (Jose,[16] a school administrator)

Questions

1. Do you hear people in your workplace using expressions like "those kids"? What kids are they referring to?

2. Do you agree with the two interviewees that "those kids" usually refers to kids with discipline issues or kids who are poor?

3. Do you think the effect would be different if the speakers said "these kids"? How about "our kids"?

4. Can you think of situations in which the use of "those kids" would not be a negative othering expression?

Activity 2: Examining Workplace Language

Collect a sample of language from your workplace, especially a sample in which people are talking (or writing) about different communities in the workplace. The sample could be a written document or a video or audiotape—in other words, something you can listen to or read repeatedly. (You must get permission before taping anything that is not a public event. People have a right to know they are being recorded and to give or withhold consent. They also have a right to know what you are planning to do with the recording.)

Listen to it (or read it) a few times. Then try to answer the following questions:

1. Are different groups of people represented in this discourse? What are the different people called?

2. Besides different labels, what else in this discourse tells you that these people are seen as different from each other (e.g., contrasts in pronouns, such as *we* and *they;* contrasts in spatial relations, such as here and there; different attributions or descriptions, such as good and bad, strong and weak)?

3. Can you detect whether one group is depicted as better than or higher in status than another? Or are they presented as different but equal? What specific language helps you know this? (Recognizing stratifying language is discussed at length in Chapter 6.)

4. Are some people framed as normal (unmarked) and others as unusual (marked) in some way? Which group is unmarked? Which group is marked? What is it in the language that lets you know this?

5. Do you think that the language people use to talk about differences actually helps create those differences or to make them negative in any way?

Activity 3: Accents

1. What different accents do you hear in your own educational setting? How are they portrayed? Which ones do you notice? What does this tell you about your own accent? Is your own accent considered marked or unmarked by others?

2. In general, how are the people with the marked accents treated in your educational setting, compared to the people with the unmarked accents?

3. Do you think that talk about accents is systematically related to nonlinguistic forms of social stratification and inequality (e.g., "ability" tracking; segregation of groups by class, language, race, gender)? What evidence makes you think so or not?

Activity 4: Language of Possibility: Our Indigenous Co-citizens

Teresa Carbó is a sociolinguist who has studied the language of Mexican presidential speeches. She points out that their characterizations of indigenous peoples are different from the way minorities are characterized in European parliamentary texts. In the European texts, the contributions of minorities are minimized, whereas in the Mexican speeches, the contributions of indigenous peoples are regularly highlighted, even with phrases such as "our indigenous co-citizens." Carbó says,

Part of the explanation for this is to be found in "reality," the 500 years of magnificent history of peoples whose level of culture at the time of the conquest was in many respects superior to that of the Spanish conquerors. This heritage has not been ignored and has been extremely useful as an ideological theme.... Indigenous peoples are presented as a scandal and a bedrock in the construction of national identity by the elite. More than is the case in most European examples, this gives rise to an inflated rhetoric in which the principles of *indigenismo* and *mestizaje* are central elements in a discursive practice that is systematically misleading about the material conditions of life of indigenous peoples of Mexico.[17]

Questions

1. What is it about the phrase "our indigenous co-citizens" that makes it seem like a positive identity (i.e., not an othering expression)?

2. Why is Carbó skeptical about expressions like this?

3. What phrases have you heard from people in leadership positions that try to give dignity, respect, and equality to a subordinated group? Do you think they help? Why or why not?

Activity 5: Language of Possibility: Who is Diverse?

Spend a day in your workplace listening to the way the word *diverse* (or *diversity*) is used. Make notes for yourself on the context and capture a few examples if you can. Then analyze what you found, using the questions below as a guide:

1. Which group or groups does the word *diverse* refer to (see Chapter 5 p. 94 if you need an example)?

2. Do you ever hear an individual referred to as *diverse*? If so, what do you think the speaker meant?

3. Is the dominant group ever referred to as *diverse*?

4. Do some uses of *diverse* appear to function as a way to "other" people? If so, what are some possible ways you could bring this to people's attention in your workplace?

5. Recognizing that the term "diverse" may be used to "other" people is a positive step in critical language awareness. Now

comes the more challenging part: What alternative or trans-formative language can you suggest instead of "diverse" as it is used in instances of othering?

CONCLUSION AND SUMMARY OF KEY POINTS

1. Othering is a way of using language to make other people different from *me* or *us*. When done in a context in which *I* or *we* are part of the dominant group or the majority and the other people are part of a minority or nondominant group, othering (usually) has the effect of making the *we* group seem normal and the others strange, deviant, or distant from the self. This reinforces oversimplified perceptions of con-trast between the dominant group and the subordinate group and also constructs a hierarchy in which one group is normal and the other is not.

2. Othering can have harmful consequences in two ways: First, when othering is done by people in a position of power over those with less power, it serves to reinforce the oversimpli-fied notions of differences between groups; othering in this sense perpetuates stereotypes and influences children's perceptions of themselves as outsiders. Second, while those doing the othering may seem to benefit by creating a normal, positive identity for themselves, this identity is fragile because it is based on the negative characterization of others. It also excludes any serious examination of complexity in one's own group.

3. Othering can be expressed linguistically in many forms, but one of the major ways is through the linguistic process known as marking. Marking involves highlighting some-thing that differs from what is normal, typical, or assumed— for example, we have the Olympic Games, which is unmarked. Then we have the Special Olympics and the Senior Olympics, which are marked.

4. In addition to avoiding negative othering, we can practice a "language of possibility" that is inclusive, uses dialogue to transcend stereotypical notions of difference, recognizes people's positive value in society, and is clear about the problems of the dominant group.

Othering takes place all the time, and we do it ourselves. It becomes problematic when, in the making of difference today, we harden or reinforce the inequalities that already exist. Through our language, we normalize the difference, the inequality, anew so that the next generation of listeners will hear it and say, oh, that seems to be the way things are. And they will go about their business thinking nothing of it because language is like water to the fish. It is all around us and we rely on it—but we rarely think about its power to shape our daily experiences and ways of perceiving the world.

NOTES

1. For recent examples, see Briscoe (2005) and Villenas (2002).

2. For example, see Briscoe (2005), Duzak (2002), Martin (1995), and Tabakowska (2002).

3. Briscoe, F. (2005). A question of representation in educational discourse, p. 10.

4. The full list of course offerings includes African American History, African American Issues, Asian American Experience, Chicano Literary History, Contemporary Hispanic America, Cultural Math, Ethnic Women's Studies, Filipino American Storytelling, Filipino Heritage Studies, Issues in Ethnic Studies, Mexican American Heritage, Multicultural Art, and Multicultural Literature.

5. For more information on these distinctions, see Van Dijk (1997).

6. For an accessible, short article on the subject of accents (suitable for high school or above) see Esling (1998).

7. A pseudonym.

8. Kotlowitz (2007, Aug. 5).

9. See Dovideo and Gaertner (1986) cited in Van Dijk, T. (1997). Political discourse and racism, p. 41.

10. *Markedness. (n.d.).* Retrieved Jan. 14, 2008, from http://www.analytictech.com/mb119/markedne.htm.

11. Chief Executive Officer—the boss, in other words!

12. Thanks to Sara Nielson (personal communication) for her insights about this community.

13. For an article relevant to this issue, see Arva and Medgyes (2000).

14. If you really want to know the answer, see http://owl.english.purdue.edu/owl/resource/630/01/.

15. A pseudonym.

16. A pseudonym.

17. Carbó, T. (1997). Who are they? p. 91 and p. 105.

CHAPTER FOUR

Disrupting Prejudice

A Communicative Approach

*You know, I'm rather dark brown and not tall. Every time
I go with my assistant, who is Sweden descent, you know,
tall, blond and blue eyes, to evaluate a job and negotiate
prices, invariably people talk to him, see him in the eye
and once in a while look at me, but keep talking to him.
This is so even when at the end it's me who signs the
contract and directs the job.*

—Mario Argueta,[1] electrician

INTRODUCTION

Being ignored, not being seen, is a social fact that occurs in real time
everywhere to most people. As Mr. Argueta's story suggests, some
individuals are blatantly ignored in ordinary, everyday conversation.
As anthropologist John Ogbu[2] discovered in his studies of urban
society—an individual also becomes invisible when not considered
as such but exclusively as representative of the social group he has
been ascribed to. Invisibility is not an illusion of the senses per-
formed by Houdini's followers, but an everyday reality we need to
reckon with because its ramifications extend over a wide range of
areas—from the personal, to the group, to society.

As a discursive practice, individuals and groups disappear in
multiple and surprising ways—from ignoring someone in conversation

to excluding the history of entire peoples in textbooks; from pushing out individuals and groups of a society's political structure to using sophisms, labels, and stereotypes.

In this chapter, we offer an approach to disrupt the pathways of what we consider the ultimate source of social invisibility—prejudice. The approach places evidence patterns (particularly numerical data) and inquiry at ground zero. We show how the use of numerical data includes more than administrative and research technicalities. The communicative language approach we outline here not only brings back from abstraction the real humans and social groups represented in numbers and statistics but also applies the power of language as a transforming force.

Here, in addition to the specific cases of deficit discourse presented in this book so far, we want to add a larger dimension to both our critique of subordinating language practices as well as to our proposal of a language of possibilities. We present the creation of different types of capital as an effective response to deficit discourses. This chapter focuses on a four-step discourse approach to disrupt prejudice: dislodging deficit discourse, building capital, assigning cause, and personalizing numerical data. But first, let's talk about abstractions and emotions.

ABSTRACTING

Numbers as used in social research are metaphors that abstract social reality and hide an array of beliefs, values, and behaviors that guided their creation in the first place. Since the 1980s, numbers, in the form of statistical data, are playing more and more of a pivotal role in decision making in schools. Educators ground many of their actions on the patterns they see emerging particularly from standardized test scores. Current official discourse considers these test scores *the* thermometer by which to measure the ups and downs of academic attainment, teachers' efficacy, and ultimately, the degree of success or failure of one of the last public institutions we still enjoy in the United States: public schools.

In this context, when grouped, the student ceases to exist as an individual and becomes a category. As a result, in educational lingo, expressions such as "Our ELL population is performing at basic reading level" and "Latino and African American boys find themselves concentrated within the first quartile in math" have become commonplace in formal and informal conversation. The use of numerical data has contributed to the creation of new schooling practices that may stay with us for the foreseeable future, embodied in our institutions of learning.

To an extent, this is what happened with the invention and use of the social security number. In order to conduct any official business—paying our income taxes, signing a job contract, filing for a new bank account, or applying for a driving license—we use our nine social security digits. These accompany us everywhere we go, all the time—we have a social security number, therefore, we exist. The only good news is that it appears that these nine digits are so randomly selected that there is no way to tell if patterns, for instance social categories, are embedded. Suppose for a moment that social security numbers are assigned by social category—and that all even ending ninth digit represent females. The matchmaking business would have a blast!

For school children, test scores do create patterns. Patterns help us make sense of what might at first look chaotic; looking for patterns is a good habit when it comes to deciding on a course of action. What we are trying to show here is the flip side of this good thing—patterns can trigger stereotypes. Whether we want them or not, the good and bad sides of pattern interpretation usually occur at the same time.

Abstracting and Emotions

Let's pause to elaborate on our definition of stereotypes.[3] A *stereotype* is a notion (usually negative), mostly conveyed through strong images we have of an individual based on our assumptions of generalized group characteristics. While some of these assumptions may be supported by an experience, a stereotype is always used to define the behaviors of every member of the social group. As John Ogbu has shown, judgments about an individual become the judgments about all members of the group. Even positive sounding stereotypes (e.g. model minority) hide a profoundly negative notion about a particular social group, as well as the other groups to whom the "model minority" is compared. If there are model minorities, then by implication there must be minorities that fall woefully short of being models.[4]

Prejudice, on the other hand, is a negative reaction or judgment without sufficient warrant about individuals and social groups, as social psychologist Gordon Allport shows in his classic 1954 book *Nature of Prejudice.* Stereotypes feed prejudice and help transform it into assumed truths about others.

Now let's move on to consider the sphere of emotions and how abstractions and patterns relate to them. Choosing how and when to act on the grounds of what the evidence patterns (in particular numerical data) show is not a simple, rational process. On the contrary, we know from our own work that such decisions are quite emotional. Emotions run high any time we look at numerical data because we know that these are used to judge the degree to which we have been effective educators, also because too many futures are at stake, as is the case with children's school performance.

Emotions, coiled at the base of our actions, exert profound influence on our rational behavior. In sum, emotions, rational thinking, and action go hand in hand, undistinguishable. Let's examine how this might happen in two different situations.

A person bleeding profusely from an abdomen wound shows up in the emergency room at the local hospital. The physician knows she can only count on a few minutes to save this person's life. The patient falls into a state of coma; there is nobody to supply crucial information on his condition, nor does the doctor have the time to meet with or make phone calls to her colleagues. The orderly, linear analysis she learned as an intern is replaced by patterns and cues coalescing at high speed in her mind. She summons up everything she has ever learned in her medical practice and school as guidance to her action. And time keeps slipping away. She takes the vital signs and applies the emergency procedures she has successfully used in the past for this type of wound—airway, breathing, circulation, disability, exposure. Deep down in her mind an unequivocal idea pulsates: She is at the ER to save human life. In his 2007 book, *How Doctors Think,* Jerome Groopman defines this moment as the point of "optimum level of tension and anxiety that sharply focuses the mind and triggers quick reactions." [5]

Across town, and at the same hour the medical doctor desperately tries to save a life in the emergency room, a new student shows up at a teacher's classroom at the big, factory-like high school. The youth stands at the threshold silently waiting. At the moment, the teacher is talking intently in front of the class, and after seeing someone at the door through his peripheral vision, he turns his head and looks at a young man almost buried under an oversized jacket, the weight of a dark blue backpack on his shoulders, fidgeting with a pen in his hands. By the time the student opens his mouth to explain himself, the teacher will have made an initial mental profile of the youth's academic standing, cultural traits, and even social status.

In the early 1970s the teacher might have said to the youngster, "Your fly is down," and according to the youngster's reaction, the teacher could tell whether he was an English language learner or not. This expression was quite popular back then and was used to assess, on the spot, male students' language competence (no equivalent expression existed for female students). This time the expression is not used. But the teacher will still follow the same principle—drawing a quick mental profile to guide his immediate actions with this particular student.

Like the physician and the teacher, we perform similar actions day in and day out, producing all sorts of ramifications that affect us and others in unsuspected ways. Our brains come up with these actions usually in fractions of a second. Scientists like Eric R. Kandel[6] propose that we make snap decisions based on tiny pieces of data, rather than on huge and thorough sets. These infinitesimal pieces of data wind up guiding our actions. The doctor at the ER had no choice but to act, and act immediately to save a seriously injured patient. The teacher at the high school, pressed by the schedule and classroom management, profiled the new student right there and then, as he had done countless times in the past. The patient will probably survive. The student probably will be tracked up or down depending of the type of profiling his teacher created. Studies on decision making agree that it usually only takes 15 to 20 seconds for an interviewer or a potential love partner to decide whether to hire a candidate or to go out with a promising suitor. Snap actions (triggered by snap decisions) are just that—fast.

Malcolm Gladwell's 2005 book, *Blink,* brings together some of the most relevant research on the topic of snap decisions. The author notes that neuroscientists believe a function of our brain located in the prefrontal cortex does the trick. Our background knowledge and life experiences play a central role in determining which factors we incorporate in our split second decisions. Thus, in the case of the teacher above, his own learning as a youth, his education as a teacher, and the accumulated experience stemming from his countless encounters with students come together at critical points. In other words, our biographies determine most of, if not all, our actions.

We stated above that evidence patterns emerging about students often trigger stereotypes, and that these almost always lead us to affirm prejudice. If our biographies generally direct our actions, then how do we alter the reproduction of the status quo? The seemingly insurmountable challenge before us consists of identifying the pathways to stereotypes. Until we do this, we cannot initiate the disruption of prejudice.

COMMUNICATIVE MODEL

We present here a communicative model that consists of four integrated actions: dislodging deficit discourse, building capital, assigning cause, and personalizing numerical data. Of course, this is a linear and too sequentially predictable proposition. But let's remember that models are precisely that—didactic tools. Here is how this works:

1. Dislodging Deficit Discourse

The first action consists of a hard, soul-searching exercise: Ask ourselves how we explain the cause of disadvantaged students' lack of academic success? This query should help build awareness at the individual and group levels. One of the most engrained assumptions among school teachers is that disadvantaged children carry deficits that need to be fixed. Let's take a closer look at this through the following numerical data statement:

> According to a 2004 report from Education Trust and another from 2005 by Education Source, the testing results in 2003 in California show that forty-four percent of the schools, where Latino students comprise half or more of the population, found themselves within the bottom two deciles of that state's ranking.

A deficit interpretation of the above statement would go something like the following: Latino children's lack of English language competence might be imperiling their testing, particularly in California schools with large numbers of students from this population, which, in turn, contributes to these schools' poor performance. This statement describes Latino children as deficit in a variety of ways. First, by only mentioning their lack of English language skills and failing to mention their Spanish language skills, the statement paints a picture of Latino children lacking in language skills. Second, failing to mention their skills with the Spanish language is also an implicit way of dismissing the value of speaking Spanish and likewise those who speak Spanish. Third, it blames Latino children for their lack of English language. Fourth, at the same time this deficit statement takes for granted the use of English in these schools and the testing system. Finally, failing to address either the quality of or the absence of language development services at these sites depicts the students and their families as solely to blame for the children's lack of English language skills.

From a deficit perspective, this is clearly a case of a linguistic and/or cultural mismatch between the school and its student population. From the perspective of the Latino community, the interpretation could read like this: Spanish language appears to be an obstacle, not a strength, for Latino children at these schools; these schools hold no responsibility for these children's academic failure.

Drawing from extensive literature, Guadalupe Valdez notes in her 1996 book, *Con Respeto,* that to explain academic failure, schools resort to three arguments; genetics, culture, and social class. While the idea that our human species is made up of superior and inferior races has been scientifically disproved for quite a long time (such genetic explanation has fallen in total disrepute in our society), sometimes it still shows up in popular discourse. Proponents of this argument state or imply that racialized peoples are genetically less intelligent.[7] Psychometrics provided the tool to support such claims in the early 1900s: the IQ! We know that not only is IQ, as a measurement, culturally biased but that intelligence is a very complex and multidimensional function of our brain's wiring.[8]

Culture as a source of deficit seems more appealing than genetics to some. Children do not excel academically given that some cultures, this argument goes, do not "fit" the school's culture! Moreover, these children often do not possess the appropriate language to understand academic speech; when a child is not exposed at home to a wide and rich range of vocabulary and linguistic expression in the English language, the rules and norms of schooling become an obstacle for this child to unlock. Worse, a child whose first language is not the dominant, official one is automatically assumed to have a cultural deficit. Quite often these children, this cultural deficit explanation continues, also come with additional obstacles—chief among these is that the home culture does not support schooling.

Social class overlaps with culture most of the time. Children from low socioeconomic backgrounds seem less likely to succeed, this argument explains, due to a culture of poverty. Children living in economic poverty grow imbued in self-defeating traditions—such as no reading and writing habits, no study and work ethics.[9] Hence, poor families' children are doomed from the outset in terms of academic prowess; it is then only fair that these children be equipped with the skills and habits appropriate to their potential (e.g., more toward basic thinking skills and, if they are lucky, the vocational and technical areas rather than the professions).

Deficit approaches will always place the burden of responsibility exclusively on the children's and their families' shoulders. This view of things is expressed explicitly or implicitly in language that takes away any possibility of transformation and hope. Additionally, this language often speaks in clinical terms (e.g., intervention, remedial) and stigmatizes children in need of support—as the children for "after school" or the "summer program"—and concentrates almost exclusively on the students who are failing and rarely on those who are succeeding.

Engaging Latino children to learn what is necessary to increase their life chances is, in the view of deficit approaches, inevitably an extra burden to the school system, not to mention the taxpayers. Understanding deficit approaches is a good step, but it is not nearly enough. We need to rely on a language focused on capital building.

2. Building Students' Capital

The concept of *capital* as we use it here operates in similar ways to money capital—we can accumulate it, transport it from place to place, and transfer it. We propose developing three kinds of capital: social, cultural, and intellectual:

- *Social capital* means negotiating social boundaries and identifying and being part of social networks. Educators, as change agents, help students learn how to successfully relate to others, how to connect to social networks that contain high social capital, and how to access (through those relations) arenas otherwise inaccessible. Of vital importance here is understanding how to deal with reputation, friendship groups, social status, saving face, peer pressure, and criminalization.

- *Cultural capital* means understanding the role of identity and the power of language in society. Educators teach students the differences in the modalities of the dominant language as it is used in formal, official settings and in informal contexts. For instance, students are able to clearly distinguish between the forms of language and other behaviors used when talking to their friends and when talking to an interviewer in a job application process. In the case of non-native English speakers, they also nurture their language of origin and their forbears as a component of their social identity.

- *Intellectual capital* means the values and modalities of learning that students bring with them that can support their dealings with institutional barriers they encounter every step of the way through schooling. These values and modes of learning stem from family and community practices—such as primary language, artistic inclinations, study discipline, work habits, and technical knowledge. Educators, as change agents, help students learn how these can be enhanced and transferred to school contexts.

Two illustrative examples might help show how capital building works in real time.

Gilberto, one of this book's authors, met José González two years ago. José was a student in a leadership course that Gilberto was teaching. Gilberto immediately noticed Mr. González's quick grasp of complex issues and the passionate tone he always used, almost as if he was in an oratorical contest, when discussing practically any topic in class. Gilberto had long, informal conversations with him on their way to the parking lot or in Gilberto's office. Gilberto followed José's teaching at a high school located in an economically depressed neighborhood populated mostly by Mexican immigrants. Mr. González always spoke with a great deal of clarity and rarely with anger. The oldest of a small Mexican family who went back from California to Mexico when he was barely two years old and then returned to the United States, Mr. González decided early in his life to become an educator. After completing his BA, instead of going into business, where he knew he could make more money, he felt that his calling was to work in his community, and education was the best way to do it. After more than five years of classroom teaching he is now a vice-principal of a charter high school serving mostly Mexican American youth.

Comparing his school to his younger brothers' school, he says, "My brothers go to Hoover High where there's no Spanish language for native speakers, and so they're marginalized." At Lick High, where Mr. Gonzalez was then teaching, Latino and Chicano kids are actively recruited for Spanish language courses all the way up to Advanced Placement (AP) classes. Mr. González continues,

> Latinos are highly successful, which is true for Chicano kids as well. At Hoover 35% Latino kids pass the foreign language SAT test, but at Lick 76% do. Of these, a high percentage is LEP kids. We at Lick don't label "illiterate" the kids whose first language is Spanish. We do recognize when they may have differences in their education because they come from rural and impoverished communities, but we don't label.

When pressed to explain why non-native English speakers at Lick High School excel in the foreign language courses and requirements, Mr. González does not hesitate to elaborate. In a categorical tone he asserts,

> I connect everything I read and do with my students to college; we at Lick instill the idea of college, and the idea of a better life. It's a constant reminder that they got to go to college. We use a language that is encouraging to the students.

When asked how this approach benefited the rest of the students at Lick High, Mr. González explains how, day in and day out, all teachers give students two messages: Do your best, and go to college. In other words, Mr. González's explicit and intentional effort to build students' capacity to deal with graduation requirements and taking and passing tests (which involves a great deal of preparation and test taking skills) targets one thing: raising college expectations. Yet, this is done not at the expense of forcing these students to become monolingual English speakers. On the contrary, according to Mr. González, at Lick High, faculty teach students how their native tongue carries added value—it represents who they are, and prepares them for college.

Giovanni Bui is another good example of what building capital is about. In his late twenties, the only child of Vietnamese immigrants, he vividly and proudly describes how his family survived thanks to minimum governmental subsidy. Mr. Bui was born in southern California, and grew up in a multiethnic environment where he easily blended with the neighborhood's African American and Latino children, to the point that instead of "Asian American," he prefers "person of color" as his social identity. He considers the family of Mario Cervantes—still one of his closest friends dating back from his childhood—his own. "We became so tightly close that I ended up being 'adopted' by his parents," Mr. Bui stated with a broad smile.

He is a bright, passionate educator, concentrated on the disadvantaged student populations, which, similar to Mr. González, he conceives as a commitment to serving and paying back to his community. Speaking of his upbringing and how it influences his work, Mr. Bui acknowledges the respect for all individuals regardless of their circumstance, a principle his parents taught him early on.

> From them [his parents] I learned not to demean anybody. I always talk to my kids about this, too. I ask them to have loyalty to each other, to their group, and not to fight among themselves and other ethnic groups.

Mr. Bui is fluent in Vietnamese, and languages have had a strong presence in his life. He went back to Vietnam to "connect with my roots, to know the people, their life, culture," he explains. When he realized that the Vietnamese language classes he was taking in Vietnam were mostly concerned with grammar, he decided to get out in the middle of each lesson and go talk with the people in the streets. He flunked the course but learned to speak the language!

When asked about the function of language in the education of his students, his straightforward approach came in handy immediately. He responded, "I teach my students that there's a time and place for derogatory language. The school is one place where it is not allowed." Similarly, when asked about helping children negotiate conflict he stated that he teaches them that "the inter-racial fights are about crumbs. Together they could get full slices."

Like Mr. González, Mr. Bui is contributing to his students' capital. He does not hide the intentions of these efforts and seems to have no hesitations about teaching students how to navigate and succeed in the school system. As social agents, these teachers operate from a clear moral purpose—students must learn how to build their capacity to remove social and cultural barriers to become contributors to their own lives and to society's future.

3. Assigning Cause

All inquiry is grounded in *attribution*—which means what we identify as the cause of a phenomenon.[10] This is very important because attribution, as a language strategy, helps us place responsibility—*not* blame—where it belongs. This approach helps us further hone our agency for change. We argued earlier in this chapter that snap decisions—judgments, actions—are common behavior among us all, and that our challenge as educators consists in interrupting the pathways leading to prejudice, thus blocking its reproduction. We also said that when looking at any type of evidence patterns, we need to be cognizant of our inclination to make decisions based on a prevalent deficit approach. We argued that capital building could effectively respond to this particular problem. Let's now add understanding attribution to our repertoire.

When initially identifying attribution we are, in a way, betting. To truly determine the cause we must do research. In other words, *cause* is the condition that determines a particular problem. *Effect,* on the other hand, is the resulting problem, or what is predictable based on those initial conditions, as in "students got high scores because they have excellent study habits." In this statement the attribution is placed on study habits, which cause the effect, high scores. This attribution could be a simple fallacy, and to disprove or prove it we would need to launch an inquiry cycle to establish whether what we identified as attribution is, in reality, the cause.

Cause-effect is a long and complex topic, better covered in research textbooks.[11] For now, we'll only say that for facilitating our efforts to work with evidence patterns, the distinction of cause from effect is crucial for assigning responsibility. This is so because once we know what we should attribute a problem to, then we can prescribe a corrective course of action.

A deficit discourse, as shown above, automatically locates attribution on the side of students and their families. A serious ramification of this displacement of responsibility might be that any potential solution is expected to fundamentally emanate from students and families. A capital building perspective primarily situates the source of the problem within the institution. Honing in on contextual factors such as teachers' practices, leadership capacity, accountability systems, a school's social and cultural life, and district policies and operations makes the institution of schooling the core of our inquiry.

Think of this as looking at obviously sick fish in a fishbowl. We want to study why fish are getting sick and dying. A deficit discourse would look only at what is wrong with the fish. A capital building logic indicates that we first and foremost must look at what is inside the bowl, not just the fish. We may want to look at water composition, oxygen, or the quality of nutrients the fishbowl contains, and also at the temperature of the room, the intensity of light, the sound decibels that penetrate the fishbowl, and so on. We must start from one point, and that is the bowl.

Educators become more effective when we take action on factors under our control, those within the confines of our reach and easily observable. We will achieve a greater degree of success if the response to, say, student-on-student violence is investigated by looking at possible discipline beliefs and procedures in place at the school than by looking at the million-dollar houses of the neighborhood surrounding the school (whose children do not attend it). Not that the latter won't help our understanding, but it needs to come after our search for answers within the school. Slicing reality this way allows us to pinpoint with more precision a sphere of attribution where we can make a perceivable difference in students' lives, a sphere where we should focus our inquiry.

Let's now look at the statistical graphs in Figures 4.1 and 4.2—and think about how they might be interpreted.

Figure 4.1   Proficiency Level Based on Economic Status

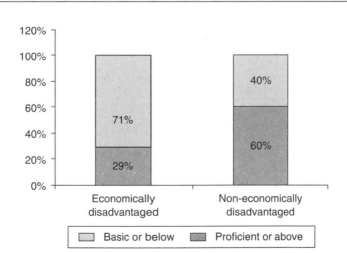

SOURCE: College Middle Academy test scores records, July 2008.

Figure 4.2   Proficiency Level Based on Ethnicity

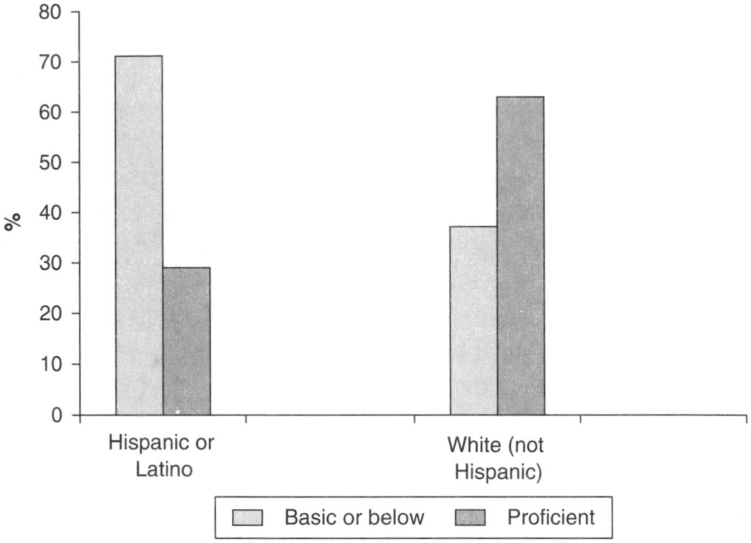

SOURCE: College Middle Academy test scores records, July 2008.

One may state something like the following:

> According to the graphs above, on average, about seventy percent of all students who are either economically disadvantaged or in the Hispanic/Latino subgroup at College Academy Middle School perform at or below the basic proficiency level on the California Standards Test.

As a second step, one may attribute the origin of the problem(s) depicted by the graphs this way:

> College Academy Middle School does not seem to provide appropriate services to the children from low income families and those identified as Hispanics.

What we have done in this statement is to attribute the institution with the responsibility for the results shown on the graphs. This inquiry approach locates the exploration of possible cause within the institution rather than the students' families.

Internal and External Attribution

We have learned from natural science that the genes of an organism determine its growth. However, we have also learned that the environment where organisms live contribute to such growth. It is the organism's capacity to adapt to its surroundings that makes it possible for it to survive. It is the interaction of an organism's genes with the environment that defines its life's prospects. To say it differently, it is the relationship between internal (the genes) and external (the environment) forces that makes up a phenomenon. This difference is important to understand so that we allocate our efforts where they leverage the greatest effect. For our purposes, as people working in large institutions, here is the key rule: *Internal attribution* assigns cause to the forces within the institution. *External attribution* assigns cause to the forces outside the institution.

Furthermore, internal attribution leads us to building capital while keeping deficit approaches in check. The reason for this is that once the attribution questions the institution, the chances to uncover social, racial, and linguistic stereotyping and prejudice among key agents (e.g., administration, teachers, staff) increase. Remember that distinguishing attribution implies the active use of language since attribution teaches us how to think about a problem's origin, what factors bring about that problem, and who (e.g., individuals, institutions) must take the responsibility for changing the situation.

From an external attribution standpoint we would then read the data above this way:

> The home environment of low-income families and those identified as Hispanics contributes to these students performing very poorly at College Academy Middle School.

From this attribution statement then, a deficit approach would ask:

> In what ways do poverty and lack of English language skills impact Hispanic students' performance?

This deficit question assumes that the academic results are determined by the students' economic poverty and degree of language competence. Again, these factors do play an important role in academic performance. And we may want to take a look at them. What we are proposing here, though, is the crucial importance of locating the issues within the institution, and not the factors external to it (e.g., economic class, student's first language), which often frame the issue as a student or family deficit. We locate causes in an area over which we have direct control as we did earlier on p. 76 before introducing the action step.

Sentence structure may aid our understanding of attribution as well. "College Academy Middle School does not seem to provide appropriate services" exerts agency in a precise way on a clear recipient, or object of its action, "to the children from low income families and those identified as Hispanics." Whereas, external attribution identifies the subject outside the institution: "The home environment of low-income families and those identified as Hispanics contributes," displacing the institution's responsibility entirely onto the student's circumstances. This could be interpreted as the school as victim and the students and families as culprits.

Now that we have seen an internal versus external attribution and related it to a deficit approach, we need to pay attention to the next step—launching an inquiry. As we stated earlier, this next step goes beyond the scope of this book, but we want to point out that what will lead our inquiry is a question. The most productive types of questions are those that guide us to look for (1) content—where we question *what*; (2) process—where we question *how*; and (3) agency or beneficiary–where we question *who*.[12] Going back to the example above, we could ask the following:

- What services does College Academy Middle School provide to its students that help them succeed academically?
- How are services provided by College Academy Middle School delivered to low socioeconomic and Latino students?
- Who benefits the most from the services College Academy Middle School provides to its students?

4. Personalizing Numerical Data

Effective communication for social justice happens if members of an institution embody work habits that help them maintain accuracy when studying numerical data patterns. Personalizing data patterns helps us avoid stereotyping the identities of the individuals and groups abstracted in numbers; to achieve this, a particular sort of culture must prevail at the institution.

Connecting Numbers to Individual Narratives

Numbers are used to summarize events and provide shortcuts for assessment and evaluation. But numbers abstract the stories of those involved in these events. Thus, the challenge numbers present is that they cannot tell what is behind them. Effective communication weaves the human texture of the story narrative that numbers encapsulate. The next three steps describe one way of personalizing data in a way that helps develop a data culture that fosters effective communication:

- *First step:* This step consists of finding faces and names of students abstracted in numbers. Group and individual students' pictures or a collage of pictures can send a powerful message to those reading the numbers. Even better, if names can be added to those pictures, the degree of concrete reality may contribute to dramatizing who the numbers exactly represent. Naturally, this approach only works when confidentiality and protocols protecting vulnerable populations have been taken care of. Not doing so makes this approach unethical to practice.

- *Second step:* Step two consists of creating short profiles of the individuals captured in names and pictures. We draw these short profiles from the perspective of capital creation and keep snap judgments under control to the extent possible. A profile, therefore, describes the contributions, skills, and intellectual strengths of a student and narrates the social relations, networks, and social status within friendship groups of each student we wish to discuss. In some cases it may be a small set of students performing extraordinarily well, in which case we may want to look at what is working with them. In other cases it may be a set of students performing very low, in which case we may be looking for explanations as to the actual effects of our efforts. In any case, we want to illuminate a larger issue and bigger group of students by taking a close up of a smaller group. The profile summarizes the student's key challenges and/or successes in terms of academic and social life.

- *Third step:* The third step consists of convening grade level, subject matter, department, teams, and schoolwide conversations where numbers, names, pictures, and narratives come together in a quest for questions and possible answers to whatever has been identified as a challenge.

BUILDING A CULTURE OF EVIDENCE

For an institution to successfully carry out this examination, an evidence culture must exist. An evidence culture is characterized by the habit of supporting decisions and opinions with empirical evidence. While educated guesses and instinct play important functions, good decisions ultimately are made based on evidence rather than merely on one's gut feelings. Numerical data are perhaps one of the most commonly interpreted and used types of evidence in schools.

Without an evidence culture nothing positive may be accomplished. Four key habits must be present for it to exist.

1. State Only What You See—
Focus on Internal Attribution

To practice this, look at the numerical data sample in Figure 4.3 and try to come up with a statement or two describing the data. Then evaluate the statements that follow. How accurate do you think the statements are?

Note in the above statements the absence of judgment, opinion, solution, or a tone of blame and guilt. Stating what numbers show is simply putting into words what the data show in numbers.

From here we then move on to ask researchable questions. To do this well, a wide range of tools and procedures can be found on the Internet, including books, manuals, and other applied research materials.

Figure 4.3   Data Sample

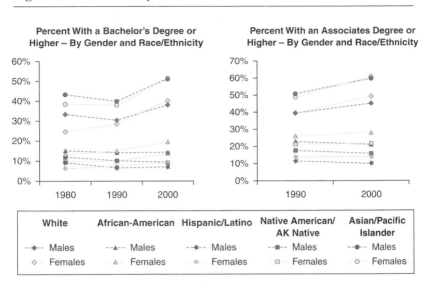

Data Statements:

Statement	Evidence
a) According to the graphs above, females between 25 and 34 years of age are more likely to get a college degree (Bachelors or Associate degrees) than their male counterparts, regardless of ethnicity, in the year 2000, the exception being Asians who are tied at about 50% attainment of bachelor degrees.	1) White females 40% White males 38% 2) Black females 30% Black males 16% 3) Nat. Am. females 15% Nat Am. males 10% 4) Latina/Hispanic Females 10% Latino/Hispanic males 8% 5) Asian Females 50% Asian Males 50%
Or b) The ethnic group with the lowest percentage of college degrees (Bachelors or Associate) for both males and females between 25 and 34 years of age was Latino/Hispanic in 2000.	

SOURCES: U.S. Census Bureau's Public Use Microdata Samples (based on the 1980, 1990, and 2000 census).

NOTE: Associate Degree Data not available for 1980.

2. Suspend Judgment

Below are three statements that might be made about the same numerical data in which the speaker is jumping to judgments unwarranted by the numbers.

1. Antiaffirmative action and antibilingual education legal actions in the 1990s in the state of California diminished access to higher education for Latinos, Blacks, and Native Americans!

2. Over the last three decades of the twentieth century, nothing seems to have helped in promoting college education among Blacks, Latinos, and Native Americans in California!

3. Since the 1980s, Black, Latino, and Native American males have become a true endangered species in higher education!

Snap judgments such as these may be quite easy to come by, but a good communicator directs the conversation away from them, because snap judgments tend to short circuit the inquiry process. People either accept the snap judgment or get embroiled in a battle over different judgments, but meanwhile, analysis has ceased. A quick move to judgment shortchanges learning and paralyzes thoughtful action. We suggest when looking at the cause of low scores of particular groups, it's best to look at school practices first. Again, effective communication promotes a conversation that fosters inquiry. The communicator keeps people grounded in habit one: state *only* what data show and focus on internal attribution.

3. Postpone Solutions

Based on Figure 4.3, we might be tempted to offer the following possible solutions:

1. In California, we must let in all applicants to universities and community colleges regardless of need and qualifications.

2. To close the achievement gap in higher education in California, eliminate all existing programs and start from scratch.

3. In California, all recruitment efforts for higher education must be focused on Black, Latino, and Native American males exclusively!

Carving from the air any answer to our judgments is the easiest thing to do. This is a dangerous shortcut to all our investigative efforts. No healthy, solid human organization will survive if its members jump to judgments and solutions as their approach to data patterns analysis. Good communication consists of guiding people toward an orderly, systematic inquiry process, where the last thing to be determined is solutions.

4. Remove Guilt and Blame

Based on Figure 4.3, we might also be tempted to make one of the statements below:

1. Lower education attainment for Blacks, Native Americans, and Latinos/as in California stem from racism!

2. The existing educational system in California favors Whites and Asians at the expense of all other groups.

3. As things stand now, as to attainment of higher education degrees in California (if projections do not change), we will soon have a virtual caste system with Asians and Whites on top, and lower castes made up of Blacks, Native Americans, and Latinos/as on the bottom much like India's Dalit caste (known as the "untouchables" in the U.S. media).

What can be said after we hear any of these statements? Hardly anything. What can be accomplished? Zero! Statements like these will only lead people to defensiveness, denial, avoidance, and strong emotions. Effective communication for justice directs talk on data patterns toward an inclusive, full embracing of institutional and individual responsibility and a commitment to finding answers and solutions. Guilt is powerful and can be very unproductive; a blaming tone is the sure path to create it. Affirming language may build an environment where what prevails is the pursuit to understand why things are the way they are.

Having the above four principles of a data culture as the guiding norms for conversation may be the most effective way to create assertive, encouraging communication for justice.

ACTIVITY: DEVELOPING LANGUAGE SKILLS FOR DISRUPTING PREJUDICE—THE SOCRATIC SEMINAR

The following activity will help develop your own language skills for disrupting prejudice:

Materials

Hard copies of this chapter

Any type of qualitative or quantitative data sets (e.g., academic performance, student work, demographics, discipline)

Procedure

1. Preseminar: Ask your colleagues to read the entire chapter and annotate the ideas and concepts they find most interesting and useful. Each participant brings at least one key question.

2. Seminar: Go over the guidelines provided by this chapter[13] and open up the discussion of the chapter content with a question, such as

   a. How do you build capital for yourself?
   b. How do you help your students create any of the types of capital discussed in this chapter?

3. Postseminar: Once you are sure participants have grasped the key points of this chapter and you believe they are ready to move on, then walk the group through the steps suggested in this chapter to create a data culture:

   a. Assign site-based data sets and ask participants to personalize the data as much as they can with names, pictures, and any other artifacts that may help participants envision the people behind data abstractions.

b. Ask participants to profile (either in written or oral form) at least one of their most successful and one of their most challenging students.

c. Establish clear and unequivocal data norms the group will follow while analyzing data. The purpose of these norms is to instill positive data work habits.

d. Organize the group into coherent small teams (e.g., vertically by subject matter or program; horizontally by grade level; by function: teachers, parents, classified staff, administration). Each team will have a facilitator and note taker, and will focus on relevant data sets. Their task is to generate at least one focus question that will ground a cycle of inquiry.[14]

CONCLUSION AND SUMMARY OF KEY POINTS

This chapter addressed the general issue of social invisibility as it is manifested in data patterns. We detailed a communicative approach as a solution to institutions' and individuals' tendency to read data patterns without questioning the way they arrive to conclusions and how this lack of attention often has the corrosive effect of perpetuating stereotypes and prejudice. This communicative approach offers four linked approaches: dislodge deficits, build capital, focus on internal attributions, and personalize data. In order to foster a constructive data culture, these approaches must always be integrated together as a unit.

NOTES

1. A pseudonym.
2. Ogbu (1978).
3. See also Chapter 1.
4. See Chapter 5 for more on this issue.
5. Groopman, J. (2007). *How doctors think*, p. 37.
6. Kandel (2006).
7. The history of eugenics has been widely documented. A good source is Harvard Facing History and Ourselves Project (2002).
8. For further study, see the works of Howard Gardner on multiple intelligences. Gardner (1983).
9. See Chapter 6 for more.

10.   The Scottish philosopher David Hume (1711–1776) was one of the first to grapple with the daunting task of cause in the western hemisphere. He argued that causal claims are always grounded on empirical reality; he also said that analytical claims originate in our thoughts and that human experience is the source of empirical claims.

11.   Manuals and textbooks on research abound. See for instance: Bogdan and Biklen (1992), Miles and Huberman (1994), and Creswell (2003).

12.   We are proposing these type of questions (what, how, who) as the best route to explaining a problem. Research in social science tends to primarily pursue understanding, not necessarily establishing ultimate causation.

13.   Socratic seminar guidelines, modified version of studyguide.org downloaded from http://www.studyguide.org/socratic_seminar.htm:

> 1.   Always refer to the text to support your argument. Your goal is to understand the ideas, issues, and values reflected in the text.
> 2.   It's OK to "pass" when asked to contribute.
> 3.   Do not participate if you are not prepared.
> 4.   Do not stay confused; ask for clarification.
> 5.   Stick to the point currently under discussion; make notes about ideas you want to come back to.
> 6.   Don't raise hands; take turns speaking.
> 7.   Listen carefully.
> 8.   Speak up so that all can hear you.
> 9.   Talk to each other, not just to the leader or teacher.
> 10.   Discuss ideas rather than each other's opinions.
> 11.   You are responsible for the seminar, even if you don't know it or admit it.

14. See Chapters 4 and 5 of Krovetz, M. and Arriaza, G. (2006), *Collaborative teacher leadership* for examples on the topic.

CHAPTER FIVE

Exceptionalizing or Democratizing?

Josephine was waiting to receive an award for her outstanding academic achievements. Dressed in her very best dress with her hair carefully combed, she was nervous but excited. Sitting on the stage with her hands folded on her lap, she could see her mother beaming proudly at her from the audience. The principal had finally finished talking about the new programs in the school and began to introduce the students who were being recognized for their achievements.

> I am happy to introduce the outstanding student of the year, Josephine Anansi. Josephine not only has the highest grades in all the sixth grade, but her test scores are the highest in the school. Her achievements are especially notable in that she comes from a disadvantaged neighborhood. If only our young people would realize, like Josephine, that hard work pays off, they too could be successful. That is the real key to success: hard work. That's it, hard work.

Josephine felt very proud of the recognition that she was receiving. And she had worked hard to get those grades and test scores, but she felt just the tiniest bit of uncertainty. She looked over at her mother. Josephine didn't know anyone who worked harder than her mother; her mother was a maid. Every night she came home exhausted from her work of cleaning up other people's messes. And each morning before leaving for work she got up early, fixed breakfast, and packed lunch for Josephine and her brothers and sisters. If working hard was the key to success, then her mother ought to be a success. Yet money was very scarce in their house.

Something wasn't making sense here.[1]

INTRODUCTION

Chapter 5 focuses on the different ways that language can be and is sometimes used to exceptionalize individuals or groups. It also contains methods of resisting exceptionalizing discourse. To *exceptionalize* is to use language to position someone as different from his or her peers and because of that difference, to position them as better than their group—a group which has been othered and stereotyped as inferior in one or more ways. To *position* someone discursively is to use language to place someone or a particular group within a particular section (usually a hierarchical placement) of society, usually in reference to another person or group. An example of discourse that positions a group of people follows.

Ms. Smith,[2] a European American principal in a low-income, high-minority elementary school was asked what she sees as the main problems in schools today. She replied, "They [the students] aren't getting what they need from the home situation. They have few oral language skills and the more diverse the home the more gaps we are seeing." In this statement, Ms. Smith positions homes, especially diverse homes (a synonym used by this educational leader for families whose accent or skin color is different than hers), as outside and inferior. She ascribes this inferiority in terms of providing for children's developmental needs. This subordinate positioning of a group is generally part of the context for exceptionalizing discourse.

Exceptionalizing discourse also allows people to discount their own immediate, lived experiences and by doing so maintain their prejudices—prejudices that can translate into racist, sexist, and other oppressive actions. In this way, Josephine's success does not alter the viewpoint of the principal. Instead of questioning her belief about people in that neighborhood, the principal sees and describes Josephine as an exception. By doing so, the principal implies that it is because Josephine is different from her group—that is hard working—that she is successful.

By this use of language, the educational leader also promotes the idea that the neighborhood's lack of success is due to their laziness. Thus, the reason Josephine is successful is simply that she lacks, or has overcome, the laziness typically found in her group. Furthermore, by exceptionalizing Josephine from her group, the principal also appropriates her and her success into the dominant group. By *appropriate,* we mean that Josephine's successes are no longer credited to her group as she is symbolically removed from that group.

This chapter examines ways in which exceptionalizing works to maintain inequities, the influence of context in the production and reception of discourse, cues for recognizing which aspects of discourse can act to exceptionalize someone, and suggestions for alternative language use. This chapter also provides activities that help develop language skills and habits for promoting equity.

We have seen how, in Josephine's case, exceptionalizing discourse presents a particular way of understanding the world that promotes academic and social inequities. The next section presents a number of key concepts for understanding exceptionalizing. These key concepts relate to (1) the ways in which exceptionalizing promotes inequities, (2) the importance of context, including dominant discourses and the socioeconomic and academic positionings of discourse subjects and participants, and (3) cognitive disequilibrium in regards to negative stereotypes.

EXCEPTIONALIZING: HOW IT PROMOTES INEQUITIES

Exceptionalizing acts on the individual, the group to which that person is exceptionalized from, and anyone else hearing or reading exceptionalizing language. Dr. Lujan recognizes the effects of this way of using language.[3] A well-known educational leader, she describes herself as a Mexican American. She was born in an economically poor border town; her parents were migrant workers who traveled from state to state in order to remain employed. Dr. Lujan is the youngest child with two brothers and a sister. She was the first one in her family to enter and graduate from college. She later went on to graduate school to earn her doctorate. Bilingual, she speaks English with the midland accent used by most U.S. news broadcasters. At the time of the interview (2002), she was in her late forties. Divorced and remarried, she has two sons. Dr. Lujan relates her conversation with the director of a doctoral program via the telephone:

> He asked me what was I and I said, "Well what do you mean what am I?" And he said, "Well, you can't be Mexican because your GRE [Graduate Record Examination] scores are too high." (Laugh.) He asked me if I was married to a Mexican maybe that was why my last name was like that....I was angry, but I think by that point I had enough sense to realize that it was his problem, not mine.

Later, she explicitly talks about exceptionalizing:

> One of the things that I am always intrigued by is how people...see a successful Mexican American woman, [or] black, and think somehow, that well, you know, we made it because we are not like the community that we are a part of. And to me it is precisely the fact that I am like the community that I am a part of—that is a hard-working community.

Exceptionalizing discourse that Dr. Lujan refers to above promotes oppressive ideas in at least four ways:

- *First,* this "exceptionality" does not disturb the stereotype that a particular minority group is culturally or by nature inferior; therefore it is "normal" for the achievement of this group's members to lag and for them to be overrepresented in the lower income ranges and underrepresented in the higher income ranges. As Dr. Lujan recognizes, "It is easier for some people to see you as the exception, because they don't have to change their little minds about a whole group of people."
- *Second,* the practice of exceptionalizing helps affirm the illusion of meritocracy. A *meritocracy* is a social and economic system where people are rewarded according to their merit, and likewise a lack of success is due to their lack of merit and/or intrinsic flaws. Merit includes attributes such as intelligence, diligence, perseverance, ethical behavior, honesty, compassion, and the ability to make good choices. In the U.S., particularly in schools, the socioeconomic and academic systems are almost always portrayed as meritocratic.[4] When an academically successful member of a minority group is exceptionalized, the ideology is maintained that the group itself is the problem, not the system.[5]

The fact that an "exceptional" person of merit from a group succeeds is taken to affirm the idea that the United States is indeed a meritocracy. Thus, the overrepresentation of certain groups in low achievement test scores or in lower income groups is due to their biology and/or their "cultural conditioning." Such beliefs mean that no changes are deemed necessary in either our schooling or societal systems.

- *Third,* to see someone's success as being due to their differences from their group (whether the group is defined by gender, ethnicity, sexual orientation, class, etc.) is to continue indirectly to maintain that their group's markers (e.g., skin color, dialect, gender) are also markers of inferiority. In this way, exceptionalizing works to undermine the confidence of those who have managed to overcome obstacles such as racism, sexism, and/or poverty in order to succeed academically or otherwise. Construing the person's minority attributes (e.g., skin color, dialect, gender, socioeconomic status) as an indicator of inferiority demands that the person either accept these assumptions as general truth or contest such notions. In Dr. Lujan's case, that contestation may only occur in her mind or in her retelling of the story in which she points out that the director has the problem, not her culture.

Contesting takes a personal toll: The psychic energy necessary for the individual to maintain a feeling of value detracts from energy directed toward achieving one's goals, like academic success.[6] Psychic energy needed to fight against devaluation becomes unavailable for learning other things—science, math, history, or a musical instrument. If you are devalued, you either accept it and despair—or you must use the emotional and cognitive energy to maintain your belief in your value. And even if you maintain your belief in your own value, there is always the debilitating pain of knowing how some others see you.

- *Fourth,* exceptionalizing also encourages others to view the exceptionalized person with suspicion by others, others who may hold positions of power. This suspicion[7] creates a negative halo effect whereby the person's accomplishments tend to be ignored and any failure or faux pas is emphasized in the minds of the observers. Those in positions of power who hold such suspicions are ever ready to demote the "exceptional" person back into their "inferior" group of origin.[8]

For example, if a man is a new kindergarten teacher—and the principal has an underlying belief that men are not good with young children—then, when the principal comes to evaluate him, the principal will be far more likely to notice negative things than the positive things, and her evaluation of him is going to be more heavily weighted with negative than positive comments. So, the man may be teaching as well or better than a female kindergarten teacher, but his evaluations will be more negative than the woman's. It is not that the principal is lying or even aware of the differential weighting of the evaluations; it's just that the principal notices and fails to notice things based on her preconceived notions of what men are "good at."

Exceptionalizing also works on a broader social scale in the case of the creation of the *model minority* stereotype for Asian Americans. Just as we saw with exceptionalizing people from their ethnic group, a whole minority group (in this case Asian Americans) is exceptionalized from all other minority groups. And this exceptionalizing has just the same effect: It places the onus on other minorities by normalizing the negative stereotypes of other groups and at the same time reaffirming the U.S. educational and economic system as meritocratic and fair.[9]

Similarly, when recent immigrants from Mexico began to come to Georgia to work in the carpet factories in Dalton, they were applauded by local business owners, who were European American, as "such hard workers," "they never complain," and so on. These Mexican workers were being implicitly compared to other workers, who were primarily low-income African Americans and European Americans. By positioning Mexican immigrants as a "model minority" in this particular context, speakers implied that the other workers were lazy and complained too much.[10]

Context both influences what we say and how we interpret what others say. Factors such as the dominant discourse and racialized academic and socioeconomic hierarchies are part of the context within which educational leaders carry out their work.

THE IMPORTANCE OF CONTEXT

In critical discourse analysis, the context must always be considered. *Context* is the situation surrounding discourse that influences what sort of language we produce and the way that language is interpreted. Context includes such things as the positionings (social, economic, academic, etc.) of the participants, the genders of the participants, the current political situation and history of the place in which the communication takes place (e.g., the U.S. Civil War has different meanings in the North and the South), and the existing dominant discourse. The aspects of any context are in fact innumerable.

Context influences not only how discourse is interpreted, but also acts to inhibit certain types of discourse (e.g., we usually do not use profanity in a place we consider holy) and encourages other types of discourse (at a football stadium we are more likely to talk about football than philosophy). The following classic experiment in psychology demonstrates how relevant aspects of the context affect the sort of language we produce.

Undergraduate men in the United States were told to say the first word that comes to their mind on viewing a projected slide. The slide in question showed a water pitcher. If the men were shown a slide of a young woman with big breasts before viewing the slide of a water container, they were much more likely to say *jug* than they were to say *pitcher*. However, if they were *not* shown the picture of the young woman with big breasts, they were more likely to say *pitcher*. This simple experiment illustrates the way that the context can influence our production of language, often without our awareness.

However the aspects of the context picked out as important by the participant (listener, speaker, writer, signer, or reader) will vary slightly according to the participant's history, ethnicity, class, gender, and so on. For example, a woman or gay man might not respond linguistically the same as a straight man when shown the pitcher after viewing the big-breasted woman. Likewise, different participants' interpretations of a particular discourse will also vary. Nevertheless, although miscommunication occurs, for the most part we understand what another is trying to communicate to us (provided we speak the same language). One of the most influential aspects of context is the status or hierarchical positioning of the discourse participants and those who are subjects of the discourse.

Socioeconomic and Academic Positioning of Social Groups

National statistics reveal inequities in the academic and economic achievement of different racialized groups in the United States. For example, in Texas in 2002, Mexican Americans ($10,770), African Americans ($14,253), and Asian Americans ($20,956) had a lower per capita income than non-Hispanic Whites ($26,197).[11] This economic positioning is echoed in the academic positioning of the different ethnicities.

The high school completion rate of Hispanics (62%) and Blacks (84%) is substantially lower than non-Hispanic Whites (92%), and the college enrollment rate of Hispanics (22%) and Blacks (31%) is much less than non-Hispanic Whites (39%).[12] These different economic and academic positionings form part of the context within which we talk about academic success and failure. In order to address these inequities, we must be able to talk about them in a way that does not normalize them nor place blame on the very people who have traditionally suffered from relations of oppression.

Although most people do not know the exact statistics, most are well aware of the existence of the economic and academic disparities of different social groups in the United States. Although explicit racism is no longer acceptable in public schools, it still exists in more subtle institutionalized[13] and discursive forms (as discussed in this book). Some say that all Americans—indeed most world citizens, no matter their ethnicity—are racist, because we live in societies of institutionalized racism. When Felecia, one of the authors of this book, brings this idea up in her educational leadership classes, students all claim that they are not racist. However, perhaps the more accurate statement is that none of them *intend* to be racist.

Felecia tells her students of an incident that occurred during her second year of college teaching: She was teaching about classroom management—about the level of discipline needed. She said that if students are engaged, discipline generally would not be a problem, but you cannot have your students "running around like a bunch of wild Indians." One of her students quickly pointed out that her statement was racist, as indeed it was. She thanked him for bringing it to her attention and then brought it up as a topic of discussion for the class. Felecia explained that it was a phrase that her mother, who is one sixteenth Mohawk, used when she was trying to get her children to calm down.

Felecia pointed out that she certainly did not mean to be racist, and neither did her mother intend to promote prejudice toward Native Americans. Yet her mother's words, and Felecia's repetition of those words, were doing exactly that. Felecia asked her students what lessons they could draw from this situation. It is exactly this sort of discourse that we seek to bring to the attention of educational leaders: how their choice of words will either promote ideologies of equity or ideologies of inequity explicitly and/or implicitly. In other words, sometimes we use a language that promotes the very things we advocate against, such as racism, sexism, and classism.

In the United States, classism[14] has never really become widely recognized by public media in the manner that racism and sexism have been (this recognition has resulted in the reduction, but not elimination of racism and sexism). However, some scholars have come to believe that classism, due to its lack of visibility, has become the new more subtle form of racism. In other words, because minorities are overrepresented in the working and poverty class, denigrating the poor is often really just disguised racism.

If we are to address these inequities we must speak of them in a way that does not normalize them. The President of Harvard University recently produced an unfortunate example of such normalizing discourse. President Summer publicly speculated about why less than 20% of the top engineers and scientists were women. Two of the hypotheses he favored most strongly for the disparities were the following:

1) Women want to have children, and as a result they don't put in the 80-hour work week that would make them competitive with their male peers; 2) the innate differences between men and women lead men to outperform women at the top end.[15]

These two hypotheses both normalize women as nonscientists and as those who prefer having children (evidently men don't want to have children). At the same time they exceptionalize the 20% of women who do become top scientists and engineers as being different from the majority of people in their group. Later he recognized that such discourse creates an environment detrimental to women becoming scientists. He then apologized:

I deeply regret the impact of my comments and apologize for not having weighed them more carefully....I was wrong to have spoken in a way that has resulted in an unintended signal of discouragement to talented girls and women.[16]

What contextual reasons may have influenced President Summers in his production of such exceptionalizing discourse? Perhaps the relative status of the participants (notice that Summers was a man discussing the limits of women) influenced President Summers not to notice the exceptionalizing quality of his talk. In addition, the dominant discourse, discussed in the next section, is very influential in determining how we interpret and describe differ-ent social phenomena.

Dominant Discourses

Given any important topic, frequently discussed, there are usually only a few prevalent understandings of the topic. These understandings are produced and reflected by dominant discourses. *Dominant discourses* are those that appear in the media and are developed by the elite[17] (e.g., those who have access to media and who make laws and policies). In studying the history of prejudice and stereotypes, one of the most amaz-ing things that emerges is how enduring prejudicial stereotyping is despite clear evidence to the contrary.[18] Such prejudicial stereotypes are produced and maintained largely by dominant discourses.

The pervasive nature of the dominant discourse often provides the background understanding we spontaneously use to interpret social phenomena. Therefore, the tendency for most is to defer to the prevailing perspectives and produce discourse that fits into the dom-inant discourse. Producing discourse that runs counter to the domi-nant ones requires heightened awareness and thoughtfulness. Such counter discourses, if noticed at all, are often marginalized as deviant by the dominant discourses.

An example of the pervasiveness of the dominant discourse is the way that most people have come to equate test scores with school success. In almost all recent discussions of public school success, standardized test scores are accepted as the primary indicator of how well a student, school, or district is performing. A primary example of the expression of this discourse can be seen throughout No Child Left Behind (NCLB)—a 2001 U.S. legislation of high-stakes testing.

Unfortunately, even in those cases where people or groups of people clearly reject ideologies of inferiority, because of the omnipres-ence of the dominant discourse they end up adopting phrasings that implicitly promote such ideologies.[19] By *ideologies* we mean beliefs or belief systems that influence the way we interpret the world and therefore the way we act in the world. Ideologies are often taken for granted so much that we call them "common sense." Think back to President Summers and his statement about why there are so few top women scientists and engineers. His statement reflected the ideology that women are not as naturally attracted by or gifted in scientific reasoning as men. If he truly held such a belief, he would be unlikely to take any steps to address that disparity, seeing it as "normal."

Educational leaders must discuss and address disparities such as the academic success of different racialized groups and the lack of top women scientists in ways that do not justify or normalize them. This discussion must include students who do succeed in the face of obstacles. For those who see women, racialized groups, and the economically poor as deficient in some way, such successes can cause cognitive disequilibrium.

COGNITIVE DISEQUILIBRIUM AND EXCEPTIONALIZING

We understand the world by virtue of our experiences; one of these experiences is what the dominant discourses tell us about that world. As we engage in the world, we build mental models of the world in order to make sense of it. These mental models include the significant parts of the world as well as rules that govern those parts. Without them we would perceive the world as an incomprehensible chaos. Our mental model helps us make sense of things and recognize significant events. Piaget[20] says that one of the ways in which learning occurs is through cognitive disequilibrium. *Cognitive disequilibrium* occurs when there is a discrepancy between our mental models (he calls them *schemas*) and what we experience in the world.

In the story that begins this chapter, Josephine is experiencing just such a discrepancy (what Piaget calls disequilibrium). She is in a moment of learning, but what is it that she will learn from her experience? Will it be that her mother really is not hard working or will it be that other factors besides a person's individual merit determine whether or not someone is academically and thus economically successful? Will it be that people "from her neighborhood" are lazy and that is why they are undereducated and poor? Or will she begin to question these formulations?

People who believe that racialized groups, women, and/or poor students achieve less because they are either lazy or otherwise deficient similarly experience a cognitive disequilibrium when they encounter a successful minority person. By *minority* we mean a group that has been systematically oppressed and therefore has less power than the dominant group.[21] In resolving their disequilibrium, these people have some options.

One option is to reexamine their understandings of a minority group. That is, they could decide their beliefs about the inferiority of a particular group might be wrong because of the example of success they see before them. They could discard their biases against that group and begin to search for other causes of the disparities. Another option (one encouraged by the dominant discourse of meritocracy) is to cling to their prejudices tightly and exceptionalize the person, thereby explaining the success of the person in such a way as to maintain and even strengthen their racist, classist, and/or sexist ideologies.

A majority of the examples of exceptionalizing discourse that follow were taken from interviews with educational leaders. However, this is not to say that these leaders were consciously biased against the groups they exceptionalized. They may have been influenced by the context to select language they might not otherwise have used. It is important to understand the directions that the context pushes our discourse, so that we can be aware of and resist influences toward oppressive discourse. These interviews occurred during 2005–2006, three years after the United States' passage of NCLB. The effects of NCLB make up part of the context as does the positioning of the participants in relation to the people discussed.

THE CONTEXT OF THE INTERVIEWS

The 2001 NCLB mandates that public schools are "to enable all children to meet the challenging State student academic achievement standards." However, schools must accomplish this without equal funding. The legislation states, "Nothing in this title shall be construed to mandate equalized spending per pupil for a State, local educational agency, or school."[22] NCLB demands that the disparities between the various social groups be brought to the attention of the public and that teachers, administrators, and schools be punished for failing to achieve certain standardized test scores. The discourse of NCLB does not blame parents for the disparities in achievement scores. However, it also does not allow room for discussing the effects of an unequal distribution of resources on schools and neighborhoods; instead, it blames the schools, administrators, and faculty for the failure to eliminate disparities. NCLB mandates that states sanction schools that do not meet preset state standards for student test scores.[23]

In many states the system of school financing is still largely based on property taxes. This means schools that serve the families who have the fewest financial resources are also the schools that continue to receive the lowest funding. Even when the state mandates equal tax dollars spent per student in public school, it rarely results in actual equal spending per student. For example, in 2004–2005 in San Antonio, the highest income school district received on average $701 in donations per student per month compared to the $169 donated per student per month in the lowest income school district.[24] High-minority, low-income schools not only suffer from a lack of funding as compared to high-income schools, but also suffer from a lack of other resources.

As Linda Darling-Hammond[25] has shown in her work, a greater proportion of the best teachers tend to migrate toward higher-income schools and school districts, leaving a larger proportion of struggling teachers in lower-income schools. The effects of unequal resourcing of schools and the endemic problems of poverty create unequal teaching environments, which all too often result in unequal learning outcomes.[26] These disparities must be discussed, both for the purpose of addressing them and because NCLB demands that they be publicly displayed and that schools be punished or awarded according to students test scores.[27]

Under threat of punishment and with so few resources, school leaders in low-income school districts often feel beleaguered. These particular leaders may be tempted to look for a scapegoat.[28] Ms. Smith, the elementary school principal introduced earlier in the chapter, spoke repeatedly about focusing on the kids and what kids need. Yet, she scapegoats families, rather than the unequal distribution of resources, as the primary reason for the difficulties she encounters with complying with NCLB standards:

> I think the biggest problems that we face today, in particular in my school, are students who come to school already below level. . . . We have Pre–K here and even our four year olds come in with some issues such as behavior uh, learning gaps. Our district has a lot of young parents. Parents that are low-income, low socioeconomic, and that has a big impact on the students. Because right now our district has mostly a low socioeconomic population of Hispanic parents.

Given the dominant discourse of meritocracy,[29] it is difficult to describe these disparities in such a way that their cause is not attributed, either explicitly or implicitly, to those who already suffer from formal and informal patterns of marginalization[30]—especially when the speaker is not a member of the minority group he or she is talking about. More often than not, exceptionalizing and stereotyping discourse such as the above were produced in the interviews of the European American educational leaders in low-income school districts.

How can we accurately present generalizations about the effects of poverty on schools and students and discuss those students who overcome a host of obstacles and become successful without exceptionalizing them? After all, to fail to mention the successes of students from "at-risk" neighborhoods also reinforces stereotypes. The first thing we need to do is recognize exceptionalizing discourse whether produced by ourselves or others.

Recognizing Exceptionalizing Discourse

We have just explained the importance of context, both in how we interpret discourse and the way context influences the production of discourse—in this case exceptionalizing discourse. This section provides some ways of recognizing what makes discourse exceptionalizing. We present three different questions regarding the language used by educational leaders for exceptionalizing. These questions include: What words are chosen? How are words defined implicitly or explicitly? Where are the silences?

What Words Are Chosen?

Depending on the words chosen, different ideologies are promoted. In 2007, U.S. Senator Joe Biden's evaluation of his then presidential rival, Senator Barack Obama, provides an example of an exceptionalizing statement due to his choice of words, "I mean, you got the first mainstream African American who is articulate and bright and clean and a nice-looking guy."[31] This exceptionalizing occurs both by Senator Biden's choice of words and the context in which he uses those words.

The most overt examples of exceptionalizing occur with Senator Biden's choice of two words, *first* and *African American*. By using the word *first* and the word *African American* to linguistically mark the ethnic aspect of Senator Obama's identity, Senator Biden directly implies that there have been no other African Americans before Obama who were articulate, bright, clean, and nice-looking. The word *first* makes it an explicit form of exceptionalizing. If Senator Biden had left out just the word *first,* it would be a more subtle form of exceptionalizing discourse. Notice how the nuance of the sentence changes with the following three rephrasings.

1. I mean, you got a mainstream African American who is articulate and bright and clean and a nice-looking guy.

2. I mean, you got a mainstream guy who is articulate and bright and clean and nice-looking.

3. I mean you got a guy who is articulate, bright, and nice-looking.

In the first rephrasing, marking[32] the African American aspect of Obama's identity implies that articulate, bright, clean, and nice-looking African Americans are not all that common. An even more subtle form of exceptionalizing in the second rephrasing occurs due to both the choice of words and the context in which those particular words are used. The terms contained within the second rephrasing are *not* exceptionalizing by themselves within the meaning of the sentence. However, once the context is considered, the exceptionalizing force of the second rephrasing becomes apparent.

Two contextual factors are relevant: First, the terms *clean* and *mainstream* are not applied to other presidential candidates; and second, the historical stereotyping of African Americans (and indeed all minorities) as unclean. By using these words only for this candidate, Senator Biden marks them out as unusual for this type of candidate. Since they are never used for any other presidential candidate (who are all clean and for the most part mainstream, but not African American), the understanding that is promoted is that Senator Obama is an exception as an African American in that he is both clean and mainstream.

Taking into account the context and the choice of words, only the third rephrasing refrains from exceptionalizing Senator Obama as an African American. The historical stereotyping of African Americans further promotes this interpretation of Senator Biden's remarks. Senator Biden did later apologize for his choice of words and perhaps more importantly, since then, he has refrained from using exceptionalizing phrases in his descriptions of Senator Obama. Since Senator Biden was later selected as Senator Obama's running mate, it is unlikely that he was aware that his choice of words promoted racist ideologies. However, it is just these instances for which we must be most alert. Sometimes without meaning to our words reinforce oppressive ideologies and stereotypes.

How Are Words Defined Implicitly and Explicitly?

Another question to consider when developing your ability to recognize exceptionalizing discourse has to do with the meaning we give to the terms by the way we use those terms. Following is an example that exceptionalizes not just by the words chosen, but also by the implicit creation of the meaning of "work ethic." When asked, "What do you think are the biggest problems that schools face today?" Ms. Barnes, a European American high school leader in a low-income school district replies,

> Some of these kids come to school—their parents don't have a high school education; so they are working two, sometimes three jobs. So the kids are at home taking care of younger siblings. You know, they just don't do homework anymore. There is very little work ethic here because kids are stretched very thin. . . . hey it's just survival out there right now for a lot of these families. Of course some of our kids that are coming from families where maybe one or both parents have a college degree, yeah and I can see it's all the difference in the world in their work ethic.

Exceptionalizing students whose parents don't have a high school education occurs here in the statement "there is very little work ethic here." While not explicitly stated, this statement implies there are some kids (whose parents lack a high school degree) with a work ethic, but they are the exception rather than the rule.

Notice the meaning associated with *work ethic*. The parents' actual labor of working two or three jobs is not seen as teaching their children to have a work ethic; nor is the work that students do at home or in a paid job considered to be real work. Here, working only counts if it is school work. So no matter how hard a student is working, if that student is not completing their homework, he or she lacks a work ethic. Ms. Barnes ignores the evidence of hard work that she herself cites "so the kids are home taking care of younger siblings . . . they are stretched very thin." The two language strategies that work together to produce the above exceptionalizing discourse are the following:

- Implication: "there is very little work ethic here" meaning that students from this group who *have* a work ethic are the exception
- Synonymy: making *work* synonymous only to schoolwork excludes or delegitimizes all other forms of work

So by implication and by limiting the definition of work ethic, the education leader reproduces negative stereotypes about working class families despite evidence to the contrary. Ms. Barnes clearly understands that both the parents and children are working hard, yet her summation is that they lack a work ethic. To make her point, Ms. Barnes contrasts the children of parents who lack a high school degree with those whose parents have a college degree, "I can see it's all the difference in the world in their work ethic."

This sort of discourse fits into the dominant discourse of meritocracy and promotes the idea that lack of a work ethic is why so many students whose families' incomes are low fail academically. It also acts to promote the idea that having a work ethic is a middle-class value, as opposed to a working-class value. It is likely that the school leader did not intend to promote ideologies that normalize and justify social and academic inequalities, yet that is exactly what she did. Her discourse promotes a bias in favor of the middle class and against the working and poverty class.

Where Are the Silences?

Talking about how the U.S. economic system thrives on economic disparities and the effect of those disparities on families and schools is a discourse that is largely silent in U.S. schools and society. Perhaps this discourse has been effectively muffled by the dominant discourse of meritocracy. It is perhaps considered politically incorrect within the U.S. to criticize the economic system and point to its deleterious effects on minority groups.

The fact that the schools in districts where families have fewer resources also have fewer resources than those schools where families have more resources is an artifact of, and integral to, a capitalistic economic system. Within this financing structure, schools are coerced into reproducing the academic and economic disparities necessary for the stable continuation of such a classed economy.[33] Silence about the unfairness of this system renders it invisible and therefore unproblematic.

The discourses of educational leaders, like the excerpt from Ms. Barnes, all too often reproduce the ideology that poor people are poor because they lack merit and that the U.S. educational and economic system is a fair one. Schools in the United States have long been touted as the means by which children are provided the opportunity to better their circumstances—and they do more toward that end than any other public institution. However, U.S. schools fail to provide this opportunity equally for all groups and exceptionalizing discourse disguises this failure as a natural product of a meritocracy.

REVISING FOR A MORE DEMOCRATIZING DISCOURSE

In the previous section we provided some examples of exceptionalizing discourse and suggested some questions that can be asked about discourse to determine what makes it exceptionalizing. In this section we suggest some alternatives to and strategies for resisting exceptionalizing discourse.

How could Ms. Barnes have communicated the idea that one of the reasons students are failing academically in her school is because they are not doing homework and that this is more of a problem with low socioeconomic status (SES) families than with middle class families? How could this be said without promoting ideologies that blame the low SES families and normalize such inequities? One way is to point to the lack of resources available to low SES families and the schools attended by those families. This approach positions the U.S.'s economic system as the problem that needs to be fixed, rather than families' lack of merit. Educators need to recognize the degree of economic inequities in the United States and the effect these inequities have on both the school and the neighborhood community.

However, if educators are to be transformational—creating more equitable and just institutions—they cannot simply wash their hands of the academic problems that are incurred by socioeconomic inequities. They need to recognize and work with whatever resources are at hand (e.g., the cultural resources of low-income families are often overlooked). Failure to maximize whatever resources are at hand exacerbates the effects of economic disparities. Mindfully choosing the language they use is one of the resources educational leaders can employ in developing a school culture that nurtures success for all students.

Creating Counter Discourses

One of the ways we can use language to resist discourses of oppression, such as exceptionalizing discourse, is to create counter discourses. *Counter discourses* use language to oppose the ideologies of the dominant discourse—for example, stories of Latinas who excel in higher education are a counter discourse to the idea that Latinas do not value higher education. Think back to Dr. Lujan's story about the director of the doctoral program and other people who see her as an exception to Mexican Americans.

Dr. Lujan creates two counter discourses in her stories that appeared earlier in this chapter. However, in order to create a counter discourse, she must first recognize that she is being exceptionalized from her community, which ascribes inferiority to her ethnicity and gender. As she describes these events for others, she creates a counter discourse to resist the efforts of others to see her as "the exception." Dr. Lujan employs two strategies in her counter discourse:

- One is to strongly reaffirm membership with her community and gender in spite of others who see her as different.
- Her other strategy is to reverse the denigrations onto the person ascribing them to her cultural group.

In her counter discourse, she also reverses the story to signify that it is those attributes that she shares with her group that have helped her become successful. Dr. Lujan's second reversal is to inscribe inferiority on those who have implicitly labeled her culture as inferior. She ascribes that inferiority to them both by the overall message of her story and in her reference to "their little minds." By these strategies, Dr. Lujan reaffirms her cultural and gender identity and resists the use of exceptionalizing to ascribe inferiority to her community or gender.

Her story about the doctoral program director is also a counter discourse to his idea that she "can't be Mexican because [her] GRE scores are too high." Her counter discourse to this story is another reversal when she states, "by that time I had enough sense to realize that it was his problem, not mine." Creating counter discourses is an important strategy for resisting exceptionalizing discourse.

Refocusing the "Cause" and Ending the Silence

In order to recognize, revise, or create counter discourses to exceptionalizing discourse, one must pay attention to

- the words chosen,
- the definitions given to those words, and
- the silences that hide unpleasant truths.

Keeping those strategies in mind, here is one way Ms. Barnes could have created a counter discourse to communicate her concerns without exceptionalizing her students:

> One of the problems we are encountering is that some students are not doing their homework. For the most part, these students have a very strong work ethic and come from hard-working families. Because many of the parents can only get minimum-wage (or lower-paying) jobs, they are forced to work two or three jobs to make ends meet. The older children in the family often must stay home to help out with the younger children or get a part-time job to help pay the rent. So many of our students are falling further behind as they expend time and energy to help support their families, rather than on schoolwork. As long as this economic situation continues, schools will have to work to ameliorate the situation. Our school is developing policies and procedures so that these students can get their schoolwork done.

By selecting different words, constructing a more inclusive definition of work, and breaking a silence about the cause of the problem, the above revision creates a counter discourse that effectively communicates Ms. Barnes's very legitimate concerns. And it communicates these concerns without exceptionalizing the students or perpetuating the dominant discourse of a meritocratic United States.[34]

In the next section, we provide activities for developing communication habits for promoting more socially just ways of talking, thinking, and acting.

ACTIVITIES FOR DEVELOPING DEMOCRATIZING LANGUAGE SKILLS

This section provides some activities for recognizing exceptionalizing language and developing democratizing language skills.

1. Get together with two or three people and role-play the following scenarios one through three.

2. Tape record what is said as you and your group role-play the scenario.

3. If you are reading this book on your own, write down your thoughts on the matter, or tape record yourself playing both roles. If you are writing, write as spontaneously as possible.

4. Once you have finished role-playing, go back and either listen to the tape recording or carefully read what you have written. See if your use of language has exceptionalized any students either explicitly or implicitly.

5. If you find language that does so, rephrase those passages so that they are democratizing.

Scenario One

You are a principal in an elementary school that is part of a high-income school district. You have just received the breakdown of your students' latest test scores by subpopulations. Overall, students have done well; however, the boys' scores in reading lag considerably behind the girls. And the subpopulations that are in trouble are the African American students and students living in families with low incomes. There is a large overlap between these latter two subpopulations. However, the student who is the most above grade level is an African American boy whose family is in the low-income bracket.

You are addressing the school district board subcommittee which has been charged with coming up with a plan for improving the test scores. How will you explain the situation to them? What sort of guidance will you give them in terms of coming up with their developmental plan that will address these disparities? What other criteria will you use in evaluating the campus development plan?

Scenario Two

You are part of a joint teacher/principal/superintendent collaboration that is going to the legislature to present your ideas about the changes that are necessary for eliminating the academic disparities between the different subpopulations of your state. Develop your presentation about the five most important points that must be addressed to achieve equity. As you develop your presentation about the changes that are necessary, you must incorporate a description of the different populations in your state and the fact that there are always some very academically successful students from each of the subpopulations.

Scenario Three

You are an educational leader and you are observing a high school social studies classroom. The students are Latino and European American, in approximately equal numbers. You have been looking forward to this observation because, in your opinion, the teacher is one of the best in the school. As you walk into the classroom you hear the teacher say,

> "We live in a land of equal opportunity. The United States is one of the few countries where you can become anything you want. It doesn't matter who your family is, what your race or gender is, or how much money you have.
>
> Look at Oprah; she grew up in a single-parent family with very little money and she is one of the most successful people in the world. So why was Oprah successful, when so many born in her circumstances are not? Here is your answer: Being smart helps, but perseverance and hard work are even more important. So if you look around you and see that some people are successful and others are not, you know that the big difference between these two groups of people is that some persevered and worked hard, and the others did not. Well, okay, some were lucky, but you can't count on luck" (the teacher laughs).

You agree with the overall message, because without hard work it is unlikely that anyone will be successful. But you are bothered by the fact that other factors (aside from luck) that influence a person's success are not mentioned and that the United States is uncritically heralded as a land of equal opportunity. You are meeting with the teacher after school to discuss your observation of his classroom. How will you address your concern?[35]

CONCLUSION AND SUMMARY OF KEY POINTS

Does all of the foregoing mean that one can never explicitly or implicitly assert that someone is exceptional?

Of course not!

But one must be careful of the words they use. Rather than saying that someone is exceptional for a woman, for a Native American, for a "fill in the blank," or as a whole ethnic group, say that someone is an exceptional human being. In this way a person's exceptionality is recognized without the downfalls of exceptionalizing enumerated above.

Pressures such as those exerted by the current U.S. NCLB legislation, under-funding in low-income school districts, and the dominant discourse create a context in which school leaders are discouraged from developing and engaging in counter discourse. However, school leaders do have resources—in particular, language—that they can begin using to develop cultures of equity through the development of alternative and counter discourses.[36] A summary of the key points made in this chapter follows.

1. Exceptionalizing is a way of using language that allows people to hang onto their stereotypes and prejudices in the face of contrary evidence.

2. Exceptionalizing discourse promotes an oppressive learning environment in four ways. It (a) normalizes the positioning of different groups, (b) affirms the illusion of a meritocratic United States, (c) reinforces stereotypes, and (d) encourages suspicion of members of minorities who do succeed despite all the obstacles.

3. Context influences the production and interpretation of discourse. Context includes things like socioeconomic positioning, the dominant discourse, and other aspects.

4. The academic positioning of different racialized groups in the United States echoes their economic positioning.

5. The dominant discourse of meritocracy helps create a context that makes exceptionalizing credible, while at the same time exceptionalizing discourse supports the idea that the United States is meritocratic.

6. Exceptionalizing normalizes the academic and economic disparities of racialized and other social groups.

7. The punitive aspects of NCLB are felt more in the context of low-income schools than in high-income schools.

8. Exceptionalizing occurs through marking particular aspects of a person's identity by our choice of words, synonymy, and strategic silences.

9. Exceptionalizing can be done explicitly and/or implicitly.

10. Exceptionalizing may not be the intention of educational leaders but nevertheless is sometimes conveyed by their use of language.

11. Recognizing exceptionalizing discourse is the first step to developing alternative and counter discourses.

NOTES

1. This is a composite of several narratives of minorities who have become educational leaders.

2. Ms. Smith is a pseudonym. The interview was in 2006.

3. Dr. Lujan is a pseudonym.

4. See Loewen (1995) for more on the representation of the United States in U.S. history books.

5. Cuadraz (1993).

6. Flores-González (2002).

7. Yolanda Flores Niemann describes these suspicions and the effects on her as a new faculty member. Niemann, Y. (1999). The making of a token, pp. 111–134.

8. Gay, G. (2004). Navigating marginality en route to the professoriate, pp. 265–288.

9. For more about model minority stereotype, see Spring (2006).

10. Henze, Katz, Norte, Sather, and Walker (1999).

11. These figures and racial/ethnic categories are taken from Texas State Data Center (2002).

12. National Center for Education Statistics (2003).

13. Scheurich, J. and Young, M. (1997). Coloring epistemologies, pp. 4–16.

14. Interestingly Microsoft Word recognizes the words *racism* and *sexism*, but not *classism*—this sort of silence tends to make classism invisible.

15. O'Rourke (2005). In this article, Meghan O'Rourke also presents the Harvard president's third and least favored hypothesis, that "discrimination discourages women from pursuing science and engineering past their undergraduate education."

16. Summers (2005).

17. Van Dijk, T. (2001). Critical discourse analysis, pp. 352–371.

18. With great clarity, Stephen J. Gould (1996) describes this historical phenomenon in regard to race, gender, class, and intelligence.

19. Santa Ana (2002) gives numerous examples of how this can occur by one's choice of metaphor.

20. Piaget (1954) is a well-known developmental psychologist, whose theories of cognitive development are commonly taught in educational psychology classes.

21. Thus, it is possible that a minority group, like women, which has been historically marginalized and has less power than men as a group, may actually be more numerous than the dominant group and still be considered a minority.

22. No Child Left Behind (2001).

23. For more on the effect of NCLB see Valenzuala (2005).

24. Briscoe (2008).

25. For example, see her recent article, Darling-Hammond, L. (2007). The flat earth and education, pp. 318–334.

26. For more on the effects of unequal funding and poverty, see Kozol (2005).

27. Rumberger and Palardy find that the best predictor of student success is not their ethnicity, nor their families' socioeconomic status, but rather the average income level of a school. Rumberger, R. & Palardy, G. (2005). *Does Segregation Still Matter?* pp. 1999–2045.

28. Briscoe's (2006) analysis of the newsletter of the prestigious U.S. University Council for Educational Administration (UCEA) found that of the groups discussed repeatedly in the newsletters, families were more negatively characterized than any other group. One of the questions the educational leaders were asked during the interviews was, "What is your relationship with the school community?" This interview question also forms part of the context in which the school leaders produced their discourse. Ten of these interviews were with educational leaders who worked in relatively high-income school districts and ten of them were from relatively low-income school districts.

29. This perspective is even more dominant in the discourse of Republicans and conservatives. This is patently absurd given the existing evidence. Recent studies (see Lussier, Greenberg, & Carmen, 1998) show that African Americans and Latinos are far more likely to be rejected for a loan than European Americans with the same credit history. And Appelbaum and Mellnik (2005) report that when given loans, African Americans on average pay a rate four times that of European Americans. One of the ways that dominant discourse is perpetuated is by high school history books. The primary purpose of these textbooks is not to present an accurate portrayal of U.S. history but rather to instill patriotism. For a variety of reasons, most high school textbook publishers whitewash U.S. history and eliminate any facts that might make the United States look less than honorable and meritocratic. See Loewen (1995) for a more complete explanation of the distortion in U.S. history books.

30. See Chapter 2 for more on marginalization.

31. Thai and Barrett (2007).

32. See Chapter 1 for more on how using the words *African American* in this manner highlights and exceptionalizes this aspect of Senator Obama's identity.

33. See for example Balibar and Wallerstein (1992) or Bowles and Gintis (1976).

34. Chapter 6 focuses specifically on other democratizing language strategies.

35. See Chapters 3 and 6 for examples of communication strategies that you might use.

36. Chapter 6 explains ways in which exceptionalizing language might be contested.

CHAPTER SIX

Recognizing and Revising Stratifying Discourse

Part of the problem of hiring African American faculty is that people stay so long in the district that few openings have come. Also, quality minority teachers are few and far between. We have seen weak Black candidates, but I would rather have strong candidates, even if they are White. There was a call by the community years ago to address this. The current minority faculty are incredible people. They are the type of people that you see the person, you don't see race. (Mr. Franklin, Assistant Superintendent[1])

INTRODUCTION

The above quote is from an interview with Mr. Franklin, a European American educational leader with thirty years in the suburban school district to which he refers above. He is responding to Dr. Evans' (a university professor in an educational leadership program) question about the lack of African American teachers in the local high school, especially given the school's recent demographic changes (an increase in the percentage of African American students from 6% to 50%).[2]

When you read the above quote you probably get a sense that something is being said that denigrates African Americans as a group. But what exactly conveys this sense?

Mr. Franklin's answer discursively creates a hierarchy, which stratifies *Whites* as strong candidates and minorities or *Blacks* as weak candidates. He does this by elevating one group and subordinating another. However, whenever we elevate one group, other groups are implicitly subordinated, just as whenever we subordinate one group, other groups are implicitly elevated.

Mr. Franklin's discourse stratifies both by elevating and by subordinating. He subordinates minorities by marking out *minority* teachers in his statement, "quality minority teachers are few and far between." Notice how the nuance of the statement changes with minority left out: "Quality teachers are few and far between." This latter phrasing tells of the difficulty of finding quality teachers, rather than the previous statement, which implies that quality *nonminority* teachers are *not* hard to find. And secondly this implication is even further strengthened in his next clause, which elevates *Whites:* "I would rather have strong candidates, even if they are White." This further implies that strong candidates are likely to be White rather than minority. Both statements are stratifying, but taken together they construct a hierarchy.

Furthermore, his statement, "they [minority teachers at the school] are the type of people that you see the person, you don't see race," implies that to see a person as African American or minority is somehow undesirable. This is a subordinating implication. This and other examples of stratifying discourse are explored in this chapter.

Stratifying discourse occurs when language is used to normalize hierarchies, to position someone or a group within a hierarchy, and/or to normalize the existing hierarchical arrangement of social groups. Chapter 6 elaborates key concepts relevant to discussing and understanding stratifying language use. The chapter then provides examples of how to recognize and revise stratifying discourse; the last section provides activities that allow for the development and practice of communication skills that build on the ones already introduced in previous chapters. The chapter concludes with a review of the main points.

Stratifying discourse is very tenacious in schools and society because it is upheld by many social practices and beliefs that make the existing social hierarchies seem natural. At the same time, stratifying discourse continually legitimizes these other stratifying social practices such as tracking—which both supports and is supported by stratifying discourse.

CONTEXTUAL FACTORS THAT
PROMOTE STRATIFYING LANGUAGE

The concepts discussed in this section relate directly to establishing the context in which stratifying discourse occurs. As indicated in Chapter 5, this context is important in that it acts to incite certain discourses and silence others. These contextual factors include a description of the socially and historically embedded nature of the two primary types of hierarchies (ascribed and achieved). The next contextual factor we focus on is tracking, which is a form of stratification that creates student hierarchies in schools.[3] We describe the rationale behind tracking, the problems with tracking, and the reasons why tracking remains a school practice despite those problems. We also briefly review the ethnically and economically stratified nature of both schools and society. These existing ethnically stratified academic and economic hierarchies tend to be taken for granted and shape the way we talk, unless they are called into question.

Hierarchies (Ascribed and Achieved)

Stratifying social practices include discourse, but also encompass other social practices that culminate in social structures known as hierarchies. For most of human history, societies have been largely egalitarian. However, over the last five or six millennia, hierarchies, as part of the natural[4] and human world, have become embedded in the behavior, psyche, and discourse of the majority of the world's societies. Although all current state societies are hierarchical, the fact that social hierarchies are a relatively recent historical phenomenon points to the fact that social hierarchies are culturally created phenomena, not biologically coded into human societies.[5]

In the Eastern World, India, among other societies, developed a caste system based on one's parents and who one marries. In Europe, more than two millennia ago, Plato in *The Republic,* wrote about the "natural" hierarchy of human beings. According to him, people were born belonging to one of three classes; he associated a metal with each of these classes: philosopher kings (gold), auxiliaries (silver), and artisans (bronze). Most readers will recognize these metals and their association with the World Olympics and stratifying phrases such as, *the gold standard.* With the spread of the Greek and then

Roman Empires, the rest of Europe became colonized by this idea of hierarchy.

In Europe, through time, the notion of a "natural" stratification of life became more elaborate, inclusive, and sophisticated. During European medieval times, all life was seen as being organized along a great chain of being,[6] the highest being God and the lowest inert metals. Every form of life had its own place on this chain. Meanwhile in the Americas, many indigenous nations such as the Comanche, were still largely egalitarian. However, between the fifteenth and twentieth century, the Americas were largely colonized by Europeans who brought along with them their notion of hierarchy. Along with the social practices of hierarchies came a vocabulary familiar to most Europeans and indeed to most of the world (due to colonial processes)—*nobility, peasants, serfs, queens, princesses, inferior, superior, laborer, worker bee, supervising, management, classy, déclassé, master, slave,* and so on.

In addition to the political structure, institutions of state societies like the United States are likewise hierarchically organized: public schools, universities, businesses, foundations, government, clubs, and so on. To view societies as inherently stratified has become normalized and commonsensical. Most of our language normalizes hierarchies as a good, if not the best, way to organize people and activities. There is almost no part of life in state societies that has not been hierarchicalized in practice and discourse. When going to work the greater majority of people in the United States expect to have *bosses* or *supervisors.* It is taken for granted that *teachers* will have *principals* who will also have *superintendents.* Religious institutions have *popes, nuns, deacons, priests,* and *ministers,* all with their very own status, responsibilities, and privileges.[7]

Hierarchies can be classified according to whether they are based on (1) *achievement*—when one's status is a result of the acquisition and display of learning, abilities, and skills or (2) *ascription*—when one's status is conferred at birth.[8]

However, these two types are often blurred together in practice. An achieved hierarchy is based on acquisition and display of learning, abilities, and skills (e.g., the doctor and the nurse or teacher and student). The different strata in this type of hierarchy are at least in principle based on the person's achievement. Thus, one's positioning in such a hierarchy is flexible and open to change as long as all societal participants are given equal opportunities to achieve. For example, one day the student may indeed become a teacher. In addition, achieved hierarchies are often considered an efficient and flexible way of organizing different activities or institutions, such as performing an appendectomy or running a business.

The second kind of hierarchy—ascribed stratification—is based on such notions as "divine right," "genetic differences of different social groups," or some combination thereof. An example of this type of ascribed hierarchy would be that, according to some religions, "Women are of the flesh and men of the mind." Another example would be the hierarchical arrangement of races and social classes "according to their genetically endowed intelligence."[9] One's status in these types of hierarchy is *ascribed,* that is understood as being bestowed by nature or god, rather than earned. This type of hierarchy is rigid and one's status cannot be changed.

Both types of hierarchies are conceived, produced, reflected, and transmitted through language. Most people in modern societies would agree that the first type of hierarchy, flexible and based on achievement, helps us be more efficient and thus is a good thing. At the same time, most people in modern societies would be opposed to the second type of hierarchy and not wish their language to normalize this second type.

So does all the above mean that it is okay for our language to normalize hierarchies as long as we only normalize the first type of hierarchy that is flexible and based on achievement? Unfortunately, there is no simple or easy rule to follow. Part of the problem is that in the real world, it is often difficult to differentiate between what counts as status based on achievement and status based on ascription. This confusion is apparent in the all-too-common explanation of ethnic academic and economic stratification in the United States, where some explain the ethnically stratified academic and economic systems as a result of different cultures that are said to discourage or encourage certain characteristics such as individual motivation. From this perspective, academic and economic stratification are achieved statuses which are open to change—if only the members of minority cultures would get it together and teach the "right" values to their children. Unfortunately, what appears to be a matter of achievement often turns out to be more or less a matter of ascription.

To illustrate how such a supposedly achieved stratification operates oppressively, let us perform a thought experiment in which Anglo culture[10] is stereotyped as one that produces "warm, easy-going, but lazy people." Operating from this stereotypical view of Anglos, teachers do not expect Anglo children to do well academically; in fact, they hesitate to encourage them too much for fear of embarrassing them. Over the years, such expectations and lack of encouragement result in lower academic achievement. Accordingly, in our hypothetical scenario, Anglos would continue to be overrepresented at the working class and poverty level. From this perspective, an academic and social stratification in the United States with Anglos on the lower rung would be seen as a "natural" result of Anglo culture in a free, competitive, capitalistic society; the emerging hierarchy would be seen as achieved, in that Anglos would have "earned" their lower rung status by virtue of their cultural values and practices (which they could change if they only wished to do so).

Understanding and talking about educational stratification as achieved due to the different values and practices of different ethnic cultures is oppressive in two senses. First it normalizes existing academic and economic inequities. Second—continuing with our hypothetical thought experiment—it justifies the degradation of Anglo culture and schools' efforts to expunge Anglo culture from students for "their own good." To sum up so far, materializing hierarchies through language—even hierarchies that appear to be "achieved"—is potentially harmful and requires careful attention. This brings us to the examination of a common schooling practice (including discursive practices) which blurs these two types of hierarchies: tracking.

Tracking

As an important social institution, it is not surprising to find that schools, too, are hierarchically organized. This arrangement may work efficiently for organizing the activities of teachers, staff, and administrators; however, it becomes problematic when it organizes students' learning through tracking. *Tracking* is the development of different levels of curricula for different students, like honors or Advanced Placement (AP) classes versus remedial or regular classes. *AP classes, honors programs, at-risk programs, vocational education,* and other educational jargon have all become part of the presumption that students have earned or chosen a particular level of curriculum and that schools run more efficiently when students are tracked according to their level of achievement and/or ability.[11] Based on these assumptions, tracking would seem to promote the achieved type of hierarchy and efficiency similar to that found in businesses and hospitals. However, there are four problems with these assumptions.

- First, although it would seem as if students could move from track to track—even the name *remedial classes* (a medical term) suggest that whatever malady a student is experiencing can be cured—this unfortunately has not proven to be the case. Once a student is tracked it is unusual for that student to move down and even more unusual for the student to move up the tracking hierarchy.[12]

- Second, as many people have noted, teaching and learning are very different endeavors from making a profit.[13] Deciding what counts as efficiency in schools is problematic. Schools without tracking tend to have overall higher standardized test scores; schools with tracking have lower overall standardized test scores, but the high achievers tend to have higher test scores than in nontracked schools.[14]

- Third, to improve what schools do, we must take into consideration social skills and characteristics which are not measurable by standardized tests that are as important as test scores—or perhaps more important—in maintaining a socially just society. These include such things as feelings of unity and empathy with others, respect for others, working collaboratively with people like and unlike oneself, and so on. So would an efficient school be one that fosters and inculcates such characteristics? These characteristics are more likely to occur in a nontracked school than a tracked one. Furthermore, tracking tends to separate students by social class and ethnicity.[15]

  How can a student learn to respect and work collaboratively with students that are unlike her when she has been placed in an academic track with students largely from the same social groups as herself? Without respect and knowledge of others who are different from oneself, it becomes difficult to feel a sense of empathy with them, let alone unity. Many sociologists have noted that one of the problems with the United States and other nation state societies is the lack of appreciation for human beings that are perceived to be different from oneself.[16] Tracking acts against the development of such an appreciation.

- Fourth, African American, Latino, and Native American students and students from families with working-class parents or poverty levels of income are far more likely to be placed in the lower academic tracks and European Americans, Asian Americans, and middle-class or higher income students are far more likely to be placed in the upper tracks than other groups. So schools with tracking (most high schools, middle schools, and more and more elementary schools have tracking) act to produce academic stratification among students, which in turn acts to reproduce existing economic and societal stratification. In other words, lower-track students end up in lower-paying jobs, while higher-track students go on to college and eventually to higher-paying jobs (which are not called jobs but "professions" and "careers").

Given that tracking exacerbates educational inequities and its efficiency is questionable, most educators who are aware of the research regarding tracking do not see it as a just or efficient method of schooling. So why does tracking persist? There are at least four reasons: First, most teachers are already beleaguered by the many demands of school, especially in the current era of high-stakes testing. Given their stress levels, they find the idea that they can teach to just one type of student and needn't diversify their approach appealing. Second, it is the way most teachers and educational leaders have been taught, and so it seems the natural way to conduct schooling. Third, despite research to the contrary, many educators still make the assumption and talk as if tracking were just, equitable, and efficient.

And finally, stratifying discourse serves to make tracking seem a logical way of schooling students. Thus, whenever educators engage in or fail to disrupt stratifying discourse they tacitly promote other schooling practices such as tracking which act to produce inequities. Tracking as a schooling practice also illustrates how the two different types of hierarchies often become blurred together and result in fostering academic inequalities that reproduce the current racialized economic stratification. The next section relates the racialized academic hierarchies to the economic stratification of U.S. society.

Racialized Academic and Economic Stratification

Many of our everyday schooling practices, including discourse, act to normalize current educational and economic inequities as they occur in the United States.[17] When Felecia teaches about these practices in her educational leadership courses at UT San Antonio, she always points out that not only are schools arranged in hierarchies, but particular groups tend to be found in different rungs or strata of those hierarchies. She asks students what race and gender most of their professors are (European American male) and what race and gender most of the secretarial staff are (Latina) and what race and gender most of the maintenance staff are (Latino).

She reminds students that when we see this sort of gender and racialized hierarchy as students our whole lives, we tend to take such social arrangements for granted—especially when these social arrangements are normalized through language. Similarly, when we find the same sorts of stratification by racialized groups elsewhere in society, we tend to take such stratification for granted. Yet, these hierarchies are not natural but rather enacted and supported by social practices including language use.

To disrupt such stratifying practices we must be able to recognize stratifying discourse and develop language skills for revising it. Ethnic stratification appears in diverse settings from medical and legal institutions to steel and tourist industries. Think of the last time you went to a hotel. What ethnic group were most of the guests? What ethnic group and gender group were most of the people who cleaned your rooms or waited on tables? What about the hotel managers? Think of the presidents of the United States and the senators of the U.S. Congress: which racialized groups and genders predominate? The next section discusses some of the ways in which language can be stratifying and how to recognize and disrupt such language use.

RECOGNIZING AND REVISING STRATIFYING DISCOURSE

In the above section, we talked about hierarchies and noted that social hierarchies are not naturally intrinsic to human societies. We also noted that for the purpose of analysis, hierarchies can be classified as ascribed or achieved. However, we also stated that hierarchies that at first appear to be based on achievement, might function a lot like ascribed hierarchies. We also pointed out how the hierarchical schooling practices of tracking act to promote inequities. This section describes language practices that work together to reproduce the existing academic and social stratification. In addition, a variety of strategies for revising subordinating language are explored.

Recognizing Stratifying Language

This section is not exhaustive in that there are more ways that language can be stratifying than can fit in one chapter; instead, it aims at giving the reader a feel or taste for recognizing stratifying language.

The stratifying language practices presented in this section include the following:

1. An array of language practices (labeling, normalizing, naturalizing, and silence) which on their own may not act to stratify but when put together in a particular way are stratifying

2. Implicit subordination by using taken-for-granted wording to ascribe different roles to different groups

3. Backgrounding through ordering and frequency of occurrence

4. The frequency of different types of representation

Strategies for revising or disrupting each of these types of subordinating language are also explored.

A Stratifying Array of Language Practices

The following excerpt from an interview with Ms. Barnett[18]—a European American, middle-aged, elementary school principal—illustrates how a variety of language strategies: labeling (see Chapter 7 for a thorough discussion of labeling), normalization, naturalization, and silence can work together to implicitly and explicitly stratify students. Felecia first met Ms. Barnett six years ago, when she was a doctoral student in an educational leadership class taught by Felecia. Felecia's impression of Ms. Barnett was that she seemed well-meaning but rather rigid in her way of thinking about the relationship between school and society. Ms. Barnett had a hard time believing that the U.S. schooling system might be systematically operating against the best interests of some student groups, while privileging others.

During the interview, when Ms. Barnett was asked about the effect of No Child Left Behind (NCLB) on students (see Chapter 5 for more on NCLB), she had this to say:

But in the third, fourth and fifth [grades] we have three levels: We have an enriched level, which is a *child who is doing fine*; we have a tutoring level, which is just normal tutoring; and then we have what we call either a MAP which is a Math tutoring or a RAP, which is a reading tutoring that we put our *lowest children* in, who are having the most difficulty.... We are so concerned, I think as districts to make sure everybody passes that you tend to teach to the *low* to move them up to just pass. And so your *higher kids* get left out, if you don't have a real strong Gifted and Talented Program.

I think one of the things that NCLB left behind is, is the Gifted and Talented Program. *I think there is a lot of kids who could benefit from the Gifted and Talented Program, if we would change the criteria to more of what the multiple intelligences that Howard Gardner has.* I think it would identify kids more because we have a lot of *gifted kids* in school, not just academically, we have those that are arts gifted, those that are musically gifted and we really don't give those kids their opportunities like we should. And then the *special needs children* ... um ... expecting them to get up to a level that is not even, I think you ought to let me clarify.

I think that you ought to give a child a chance to go as far as they can go. *But I think you also have to recognize that there are some kids that aren't ever going to make it there. And, and a law isn't going to change that, because you are dealing with human beings.* You are not dealing with robots and so I think your *lower children* and *upper children* are the losers when you have a program like No Child Left Behind. [Italics are added to point out pertinent phrases.]

The two points we want to focus on in the above citation are (1) her uneasiness and ambivalence about the fairness of tracking,[19] and (2) her use of specific labels that act to normalize tracking and naturalize the existing academic hierarchy.

Ambivalence About Tracking

Ms. Barnett seems to be struggling with some issues of equity when she discusses the Gifted and Talented Program, but at the same time she discursively reproduces the ideology of a natural academic hierarchy. In fact, she even contradicts herself. First she says, "We are so concerned, I think as districts to make sure everybody passes that you tend to teach to the low to move them up to just pass." However, later she contradicts herself with "so I think your lower children and upper children are the losers when you have a program like No Child Left Behind." It is difficult to tell whether she thinks the children who are perceived as low achievers are being under or over served by public schools.

In addition, Ms. Barnett realizes that the Gifted and Talented Program fails to include many children who ought to be part of it, and thus that it might be flawed in such a manner so as to systematically exclude certain children: "I think there are a lot of kids who could benefit from the Gifted and Talented Program, if we would change the criteria to more of what the multiple intelligences that Howard Gardner has."

Her ambivalence may indicate a rethinking of her ideas about tracking and hierarchies of abilities, and she might be in the process of changing the way that she talks to better reflect her changing understanding. Nevertheless, she directly endorses the idea of natural hierarchies when she says: "I think you also have to recognize that there are some kids that aren't ever going to make it there. And, and a law isn't going to change that, because you are dealing with human beings." In this text she explicitly naturalizes the existing hierarchies—that is, she makes it an immutable fact of human beings and, in particular, students.

Normalizing and Naturalizing
Student Tracking Through Labeling

The normalization of tracking and naturalization of an academic hierarchy occur throughout Ms. Barnett's discourse about the children who are placed in different academic levels (i.e., tracks); she repeatedly marks out students using labels such as *lowest children, lower children, higher children, gifted children, special needs children,* and *upper children.* The only exception occurs in her statement, "We have an enriched level, which is a child who is doing fine." In this one example she constructs a more holistic way of understanding the child's achievement and that the child "is doing fine" leaves an opening for other aspects of the child's identity.

Using labels to refer to students in and of itself alienates and narrows students' identities to one particular aspect. However, in addition to narrowing the child's identity, the particular sort of labeling used by Ms. Barnett not only makes the children's achievement level the whole of their identity, it also implies that the level of achievement is inherent to the child, not a product of schooling experiences.

Selective Silence as Part of Stratifying Discourse

Another aspect of her discourse on this topic is her silence— what she doesn't say. There is a wealth of research and statistics pointing to the fact that academic stratification is marked by class and ethnicity (see Chapter 5 for specific statistics). By remaining silent or failing to question this academic phenomenon, Ms. Barnett further naturalizes the existing academic hierarchy— that is, she doesn't question why it is that in the United States (as well as many other countries) certain ethnicities and economic classes are far more likely to be the "kids that aren't ever going to make it."

The text from Ms. Barnett's interview illustrates how stratifying occurs through an interweaving of language strategies. The sheer frequency of her hierarchical labeling as seen in her discourse strengthens the stratifying effect. Stratifying language also occurs more simply through subordination.

Subordination

Subordination through language occurs when language is used to position someone or a group as less than another individual or group, or deficit in some way. The excerpt at the beginning of this chapter gave an example of how marking out certain aspects of a person's identity could act to subordinate them or elevate them. Subordination by language is a type of stratifying discourse. Mr. Cortez[20] uses language in this manner.

Mr. Cortez grew up in the low-income neighborhood where his current school is located, but he no longer lives in that neighborhood. His children are full-grown, and he has recently divorced and remarried. He became a middle school principal for the first time two years before the interview. Before that, he was an assistant principal at an elementary school.

At the time of the interview, he was still struggling with learning the ropes and frustrated with the fact that other principals were not keen on sharing strategies that they used to lead their schools. Mr. Cortez has dedicated his career to ensuring that Mexican American children and indeed all children are given the educational opportunities they need in order to succeed academically, socially, and economically. He is committed to the educational well being of the students in his school.

For him, the biggest problem with schools today are single parent families. He claims that because of the growing numbers of single parent families, especially in low-income neighborhoods, there is an extreme need to focus on the boys in his school. When Felecia asked him why he felt it was so important to focus on the boys, this is what he had to say:

> I think for some of the boys. . . . Not having that, not having the dad, you know, not to sound cliché or anything but they need to get the concept of being the provider, the concept of being the protector of the family.

In this text, Mr. Cortez struggles to articulate the particular importance of helping boys. Perhaps he understands in some way that he is implicitly subordinating the needs of girls to that of boys and that he is upholding patriarchal values. His hesitation is shown when he refers to the clichés of boys needing to learn the concept of being providers and protectors of the family.

Mr. Cortez's use of language clearly normalizes the male dominance.[21] His use of the definite article, *the* in front of "concept of being the protector of the family" makes "males as protectors" into something that is already assumed by both him and the listener, that is, as something that does not need to be explained or questioned. It is a given. Furthermore, using the definite *the* instead of the indefinite *a* suggests that the father is the *only* protector and provider— negating the possibility that these roles be shared with the mother. Much of our stratifying language acts covertly or beneath the level of awareness to support an ideology of a hierarchy in which particular groups of people are subordinate to others. Two of the ways in which groups are subordinated more covertly is by backgrounding and frequency of representation.

Backgrounding and Foregrounding

Backgrounding is using language to position a person, group, or topic as less important. *Foregrounding* is the opposite and means to position a person, group, or topic as more important. Backgrounding and foregrounding always occur simultaneously. Backgrounding and foregrounding occur through grammar, but when this happens it usually happens on a conscious basis, and our research found little evidence of stratifying grammar used to promote ideologies of inequities in the discourse of educators. An example of this would be, "While six students failed the test, a majority of the students passed," compared to, "While a majority of the students passed, six students failed." In the first sentence the six failing students are backgrounded compared to the overwhelming majority that passed. In the second sentence, the six students who failed are foregrounded over the majority who passed. The order in which one group appears in comparison to other groups also acts to foreground one and background the others.

Backgrounding and Foregrounding Through Order

The order in which a topic or group of people appears in a list acts to foreground or background, whether the order in a sentence, a paragraph, a paper, or a book. People, groups, items, or anything positioned at the beginning are typically seen as more important or relevant, while those at the end of the list are perceived as less important or less representative of the list. So for example, if I were to list the different ethnicities in my classroom as African American, Japanese American, Latino, European American, and American Indian, African American would be foregrounded as the most important ethnicity, while American Indian would be backgrounded as least important. Similarly, when writing a paper or giving a talk, the first topic addressed is typically seen as the most important, while the last topic addressed is perceived as the least important.

If we are ever to list or discuss various ethnicities, they must appear in some order. Inevitably one ethnicity will be foregrounded and another backgrounded in any list or even in any paper or talk in which more than one ethnicity is discussed. So does that mean in any one sentence where we list social groups and in any talk about more than one group of people that we must always background some ethnicities more than others? Yes. Two language strategies, colorblindness and alphabetizing, are sometimes used to get around this difficulty. However there are problems with both language strategies.

Revising Discourse That Stratifies Through Order

A number of different strategies have been developed and used by educators who are trying to avoid stratifying groups through order. This section examines these language strategies.

Colorblind Discourse?

One recent language strategy used by many educators is to adopt a discourse of colorblindness and gender blindness; in other words, the discourse fails to recognize any different ethnicities or any other social group.[22] Instead all cultures are seen as sharing universal human traits. Educators sometimes use this language strategy under the belief that the conscious avoidance of ethnic or racial terms will act to eliminate the prejudice, bias, and stereotypes of the various groups that have been oppressed.

At the beginning of the chapter, we saw this quote from Mr. Franklin, a suburban assistant superintendent: "The current minority faculty are incredible people. They are the type of people that you see the person, you don't see race." This text advocates a strategy of colorblindness in that Mr. Franklin implies that being oblivious of an African American's race is a good thing. And in her interviews of principles of public schools, one of the authors, Rosemary,[23] found that many principals also sought to use a *color-blind* strategy, a refusal to recognize racialized identities as a factor in their analyses and policies. However there is a major problem with adopting this language strategy.

Rosemary notes that principals used this strategy with the belief that positive group interrelations can be attained if we refuse to "see" ethnicity or race. By doing so, people believe that they will be able to treat everyone fairly. But there is a problem with this notion. Being colorblind means being blind to how different ethnicities experience the world. The blindness has two very negative results. First, it is unlikely that understanding and empathy will ever develop between different ethnic groups if discourse is colorblind. Second, blindness to the different experiences means being blind to the injustices and inequities that occur along lines of color and ethnicity. Being gender blind also has the same sort of negative effects. Another strategy commonly used to avoid fore- or backgrounding in listing people is that of alphabetizing.

Alphabetizing?

Ordering people or groups alphabetically really doesn't work. Ask any person who has a last name beginning with a *Z* and who has gone through the U.S. schooling system. Even though students were ostensibly organized by alphabet so as to avoid the appearance of favoring one person over the other, nevertheless, the person whose last name begins with *Z* is always being positioned last, which connotes as the least important.

So far we have explored the problems inherent in three language strategies that people have used in the hope that they will not subordinate or background groups that have been historically oppressed. But do not despair; there are language strategies that can be used to avoid backgrounding by order.

Variation of Order!

In order to avoid stratifying through backgrounding, we suggest varying the order in which ethnicities or other groups are listed or discussed. And if in doubt, we suggest listing first those ethnicities or groups that have historically been marginalized. This habit is easy to develop if one just pays attention to the order in which one lists groups or people. When writing something such as a memorandum or notes for a talk, after you finish a draft, go through and make sure that you have varied the order in which groups or people appear. When in doubt, try to foreground and background groups in a manner that disrupts stereotypes. For example, when talking about the shapers of U.S. history, begin your sentence or talk with women and ethnic minorities rather than the traditional European American males. Backgrounding/foregrounding is just one way subordination occurs; groups can also be subordinated by their overall frequency and type of representation in discourse.

Frequency and Type of Representation

Another way of subordinating one group to another is the relative frequency in which groups appear in discourse and under what circumstances they appear in discourse. When you think of someone on welfare in the United States, who comes to mind? What ethnicity? What gender? If you were to be statistically accurate, it would be a European American woman. There are more European American women on welfare in the Unites States than any other gender/ethnicity. If a different ethnicity or gender comes to mind, that is probably because in the U.S. media a different ethnicity is more often linked with welfare than the group (i.e., European American women) whose members outnumber others' on welfare.

What sort of names appear most often in everyday classroom language use such as story problems or examples of artists or scientists? The ethnicity and gender associated with those names will become the ones students associate with artists, politicians, scientists, and so on. In this way a discursive hierarchy is enacted in which those on the top are those who come from the ethnicities most frequently positively represented in the discourse of teachers and textbooks.

Disrupting Language That Stratifies by Frequency or Association

We offer three approaches to language that an educational leader might use to disrupt language that normalizes existing academic and social stratification. The first two linguistic approaches help us avoid such stratifying language. The third approach suggests a way of disrupting stratifying language.

The first of these approaches is simply to take care that names of all ethnicities and both genders appear approximately equally often in their discourse and that of teachers. The second of these approaches is to ensure that when we are talking or writing about something negative or positive, we make sure to include all groups approximately equally. Again if one is unsure about how often or in what way different groups have been represented or associated, always choose the representation or association that runs counter to stereotypes.

The third approach is to problematize the discourse of anyone who engages in stratifying by frequency or representation. The next section gives an example of how Mr. Norte, an educational leader introduced in Chapter 1, problematizes the use of stratifying metaphors. The next section also provides some activities that will help the reader develop intellectual habits for transforming stratifying discourse.

ACTIVITIES: DEVELOPING LANGUAGE HABITS FOR SOCIAL JUSTICE

The following activities are designed for two to four people to practice developing the intellectual habits that disrupt stratifying.

Activity 1: Minding Your Metaphors

Rosemary was observing a staff development session led by an educator, Mr. Norte, who has successfully advocated for social justice in the schools he is responsible for. Next is her description of one episode.

Mr. Norte had written down on the board one of the contributions a teacher had made about "agenda items" for future sessions. The teacher had said something like "We need to create a master calendar." Mr. Norte wrote *master calendar* on the board, but then paused and said to the group, "Hmm, somebody help me think of a better word for that." He didn't mean right at that moment but in the future. It was more like noticing that there was a problem with the word *master*, and doing so out loud in a way that invited others into the thinking process. Notice that this could easily have been an occasion for "language police" type of activity. He could have said to the woman who spoke, "I have a problem with that word. Can you change it?" But this would place the onus on her, rather than on the whole group. And it would no doubt make her reluctant to speak again.

Think of phrases or sentences that, as in the above scenario, act to normalize hierarchies. Try to come up with various ways of disrupting the use of such phrases. When devising these strategies, try, as Mr. Norte did above, to do so in a way that does not create blame or shame. If you have difficulty doing this, review the suggestions in Chapter 4 for avoiding blame or shame.

Activity 2: Revising Stratifying Language

As a group, go back in this chapter to the excerpt from Ms. Barnett's interview. First, determine which parts of the excerpt explicitly state ideologies that promote stratification by ascription. Cross out all of those phrases. Next, decide which of the sentences are dealing with topics that you think need discussion in order to understand how the high-stakes testing, like that mandated by NCLB, are affecting students. Then individually revise those sentences so that they are not stratifying. Share your revisions with each other, and discuss the merits and problems with each of the revisions that people came up with individually.

Activity 3: Developing Your Own Alternatives

Look at our suggestions for recognizing and revising stratification by backgrounding and foregrounding. Can you think of other language strategies that might be used to avoid this sort of stratification? Evaluate the merits of and the problems with strategies that you consider.

Activity 4: Building Localized Language Awareness

Find a report about diversity written by your local school district. Evaluate this report for stratifying language use.

1. What groups are mentioned in the report? Does it subordinate any group consistently? By order? By frequency of representation? By type of representation?

2. Are labels or acronyms used in such a way as to normalize tracking?

3. Is academic stratification normalized by strategic silence?

4. Is the text colorblind or gender blind?

5. Can you find any other language strategies that work independently or together to stratify?

CONCLUSION AND SUMMARY OF KEY POINTS

In Chapter 6 we looked at aspects of the context found in many nation states that act to incite stratifying discourse. Of all the oppressive language practices we have discussed, stratifying is perhaps the most nuanced, because many of us believe that organizing our social institutions hierarchically is a necessary or even a good thing. At the same time, we believe that normalizing the existing racialized academic and economic hierarchies is contrary to our ideals of equity and social justice. Thus, we must be ever alert to differentiate language that promotes ascribed hierarchies but not achieved hierarchies. And all too often, it proves difficult to tell the difference. But unless we, as educational leaders, learn to tell the difference and disrupt ascribed hierarchies, we jeopardize our other efforts for equity and social justice. A summary of the key points of this chapter follows.

1. Stratifying language naturalizes and/or normalizes the idea of academic, social, and economic hierarchies and/or positions someone or a group so as to normalize existing hierarchies.

2. Social hierarchies are not intrinsic to human society, although they are universal among nation states (i.e., highly organized political units with centralized governments).

3. Hierarchies can be classified as (a) based on achievement or (b) based on ascription. In practice these two types of stratification often become blurred.

4. Currently, in the United States as well as many other countries, academic stratification according to class and ethnicity exists.

5. Tracking is a schooling practice that reproduces traditional academic and economic hierarchies. Tracking is promoted by stratifying language.

6. Stratifying occurs by subordination, when one group is subordinated to another in terms of importance or worth.

7. Stratifying language can also occur through a complex of language strategies such as labeling, silencing, naturalizing, and normalizing.

8. Stratification also occurs by backgrounding and foregrounding (by order, by frequency of representation, and by discursive associations).

9. Variation of order, frequency, and type of association offer an approach for revising stratifying language use.

10. Respectfully problematizing the use of stratifying words or phrases can help disrupt stratifying language.

As we noted earlier in the chapter, we have not examined all the ways in which we stratify through language. Chapter 7 examines at length one way in which subordination or stratification occurs through the use of deficit labeling.

NOTES

1. Evans, A. (2007). School leaders and their sensemaking about race and demographic change, pp. 139–188.

2. Evans (2007). Mr. Franklin also adopts a policy of color blindness. The problems with adopting a color blind attitude have been discussed at length by a number of scholars. See for example Henze (2005).

3. The hierarchical nature of schooling in the United States was relatively undeveloped until the beginning of the twentieth century, during which time schools began to pattern themselves after businesses.

4. See Haraway (1991) for more about how nature has been interpreted as patriarchal and hierarchical and how new nonhierarchical interpretations are beginning to emerge.

5. Nanda and Warms (2004).

6. De Valades (1579).

7. One can see how hierarchy in organizations has become the normalized, accepted practice if we take a close look at the language used to describe nonhierarchical organizations (or organizations with fewer layers of hierarchy): they are called *flat organizations*—usually meaning that there is a director of some kind, and everybody else is of equal status. The word *flat* marks this type of organization as unusual; the unmarked form–organization—needs no descriptor because it is assumed to be hierarchical.

8. For more on the differences between hierarchies based on achievement or ascription see Chapter 7 in Mukhopadhyay, Henze, and Moses (2007). *How real is race?*

9. A recent example of someone setting up such a hierarchy can be seen in Herrnstein and Murray (1994). An historical account of the construction of such hierarchies is provided by Gould (2001).

10. Anglo Americans are a subset of European Americans that is distinctly different from, say, Italian Americans.

11. See Spring (1976) for more on schools and the cult of efficiency.

12. For a detailed examination of tracking, see Oakes (2005).

13. Despite repeated analogies by many, who liken students' standardized test scores to business profits.

14. Oakes (2005).

15. Oakes (2005).

16. This phenomenon is readily observable if one watches U.S. news coverage of the Iraq war. U.S. casualties are always catalogued, while Iraqi casualties are seldom if ever mentioned.

17. Anyon, J. (1981). Social class and school knowledge, pp. 3–42.

18. A pseudonym.

19. Interestingly, one of the topics of that class was the historical and current problems of gifted and talented programs. For more on this topic, see Gabbard (2000).

20. A pseudonym.

21. In terms of subordinating social practices, Marx pointed to the subordination of women as the first consistent type of social subordination. For more on this, see Marx, K. (1951). The woman question, pp. 5–37.

22. Henze, R. (2005). Metaphors of diversity, intergroup relations, and equity in the discourse of educational leadership, pp. 243–267. See also Rusch, E. (2004). Gender and race in leadership preparation, pp. 14–46. Or see Briscoe (2006). This discursive avoidance of race and ethnicity, especially in regard to their differential positioning within schooling, has also been noted in educational programs in Britain. See Bowl (2003).

23. Henze (2005).

CHAPTER SEVEN

Contesting Deficit Labels

> Once a teacher labels a student "low achiever" another teacher will take it for granted. It creates a continuum of perception of the student as low achiever. When teachers differentiate instruction they assign the kid to lower level work, they may ask the kid to stay there cutting paper, and the kid won't pass the CAHSEE.[1] (José Gonzalez, social studies teacher at Lick High School)

INTRODUCTION

We would find it difficult to convey thought, to establish a relationship with our surroundings, and to make sense of daily experience without language and its structures and categories. How is labeling part of it? All human institutions and organizations—such as schools, hospitals, the manufacturing plant, and the office—need categories specific to their functions as a way to infuse some order into an otherwise messy existence.

For instance, schools have categories to define the functions and work of adults and children: administrators, teachers, classified staff, students, all of which signify a job title, a profession, or a role. Stated this way, no negative connotation is attached. Yet within a certain context, each of these names may take different meanings and carry different values. In an adversarial school climate, for example, teachers will deride whoever expresses interest or enrolls in a leadership preparation program with expressions such as "you have moved to the dark side." *Administrator* takes here a negative meaning.

While the origin of a label may simply respond to the need to rationalize social interactions, some may become a means of assigning shortcomings and deficits to those to whom the labels are applied. Being a school administrator is a respectable job and title; it only becomes a put-down within a specific context. We have never heard school people in general hurling the word *administrator* at each other with the intent to hurt.

The frequent use of a category (e.g., that once might have been coined as a clinical signifier of a concrete behavior, English language competence, or physical challenge) might change it into a commonly and uncritically accepted name. That is the case with many of the psychological terms that entered into the field of teaching via special education, such as *attention deficit disorder.*

Labels embody moral values because through them people express both their perceptions and expectations of the individual and/or the group thus named. In the quote above, Mr. Gonzalez cautions us about the risk of labeling as a habitual, accepted way adults talk because talking always has an impact on the life of the individual and groups talked about. Deficit labels are an example of subordinating language, which as we have seen in Chapter 6, act to stratify society. For example, deficit labels create low expectations. Low expectations will very likely produce low-performing students. The problem with that is, as Mr. Gonzalez points out, once a label (such as *low-performance kid*) is applied, it usually follows the student everywhere and affects this student's life chances for a long time to come. This chapter focuses on the habits and talk practices of educators that effectively redress the cultural effects of deficit labels.

REDRESSING DEFICIT LABELS: HABITS AND CHALLENGES

In their study, Troyna and Hatcher[2] noted that utterances have two functions—expressive and instrumental—which are not always congruent to one another. The authors explain how sometimes we say what we believe in, and other times we just say what first comes to mind, with no convictions attached. In this study the researchers discovered how some children would express racist beliefs through openly derogatory labels. This is an example of the *expressive function of language.* They also found that at times children would use racist language without holding racist beliefs. This is an example of the *instrumental function of language.*

While the researchers realized that in both cases the intent was to hurt, in the latter situation the intent did not coincide with the children's actual belief system. This distinction is critically important to keep in mind because the approaches for dealing with situations of this sort may differ considerably. Reeducating a person who uses openly derogatory labels but who does not believe what he or she is saying presents a different set of challenges than confronting a person whose utterances and beliefs are one and the same.

Gilberto, one of the authors of this book, conducted a qualitative study of twenty-seven educators combining in-depth interviews, a survey, participant/observer techniques, and a focus group of seven.[3] His study showed that these educators tended to experience a constant push and pull between their understanding of the power of daily talk and their willingness and skills to do something about it.

In the following two sections, we show how these educators struggle through constant effort to redress the negative and debilitating effects of labeling and the challenges raised by the tension between instrumental and expressive functions of language.

Self-Monitoring and Substitution

Ms. Darbi Pannell was widely respected as one of the most dedicated and thorough social studies teachers at College Academy Middle School. Her knowledge of the subject matter and her innovative, student-centered teaching methods made her popular among students and inspiring to many of her colleagues. In her middle thirties and a mother of two school children, Ms. Pannell appeared to possess a strong understanding of what it takes to promote equitable education in a diverse population. When Gilberto first met her, she had already made up her mind about her leadership. She wanted to transcend the borders of the classroom. By the time of this writing she had become an administrative leader at her site.

Her response encapsulates what most survey participants said to a question exploring the use of labels normally used to classify students. The question was "What do you typically do when using labels?" She wrote, "I usually catch myself before the words fly out of my mouth. Then I rephrase—not to be politically correct (so much of that is nonsense!), but to avoid insulting and demeaning someone" (Darbi Pannell, assistant principal, College Academy Middle School).

Self-monitoring and language substitution often operate simultaneously. Self-monitoring one's utterances is the first clear indication people understand the potential subordinating role of language. Substituting subordinating language with positive language in daily communication occurs only when we have some degree of self-monitoring. Self-monitoring is not easy, though. We are so habituated to using terms, expressions, and all the linguistic devices available that, over time, we tend to take language for granted. Yet as we show here, self-monitoring is not only possible but necessary as the first stepping stone in the path to ridding our daily talk of deficit labels.

Ms. Pannell's "catching" herself clearly shows self-monitoring. She is unknowingly distinguishing the instrumental from the expressive functions of language in that she does not want her language to be "insulting and demeaning someone." She seems to clearly be acting out of a sense of what is morally acceptable or unacceptable—that saying something at an inappropriate place and moment will negatively impact others. In other words, self-monitoring and substitution contribute to closing the gap between true beliefs and daily talk. One of the study's open questions was concerned with labels that help organize work. Most participants agreed that they avoid deficit labeling as much as possible. They acknowledged replacing them with either new, less charged descriptors or with explanations.

While a good step forward, self-monitoring and substitution do not necessarily imply a questioning of one's deep-rooted assumptions. To go to this deeper level, we need to first clarify the difference between what we do and what we say we do. To shed some light on this point, let's see what Ms. Lupe Vasquez, an English language teacher at Hills Middle School, said in a series of interviews.

The interviews always took place immediately after her students left for home. The soft light of the spring afternoons enhanced the tones of her seemingly chaotic classroom. Books everywhere, a dormant computer at one corner, butcher paper on the walls, a projector and three easels standing in the middle as if readily waiting for her instructions. "The kids just left," she often said, meaning: "the mess is not mine." Gilberto, the interviewer, understood her explanations. When he was teaching high school, his classroom looked like a train wreck at the end of the last class, and he felt proud of it because he considered it the result of high creativity and student engagement.

Ms. Vasquez was one of the most senior teachers at her site and a veteran of the Cesar Chavez mobilizations in California's central valley. This early life experience marked her career path. After being a community organizer and activist for the United Farm Workers Union, she decided to go to college to become a teacher. Since then, she never left the classroom. Here is an excerpt from one of the interviews in which she discusses "catching herself":

> I recognize my biases and I make an effort to correct them. I am able to screen what I am about to say out and notice when it will project an image of myself that is not who I am. At times I don't catch myself and my brother catches it for me and points out the irony of what he believes I think I stand for and what I had just said! He provides honest feedback, which I welcome.

In the 1974 book *Theory in Practice*, Chris Argyris and Donald Schön note that we guide our actions following our own mental models (sometimes mental models of which we are unaware) rather than the ideas we use to explain those very actions. In other words, our actions do not always match our beliefs.

The authors explain that such dissonance means that our actions may follow a logic that has little to do with the rationale we deploy when explaining those actions to ourselves and to others. Argyris and Schön further explain that we operate using two distinctive theories of action: one, "in-use," which is the story our actions tell, and another, "espoused," which is the story of our actions we tell to ourselves and to the world. Hence, our actions and beliefs may sometimes be inconsistent with one another.

This apparent incoherence does not mean that our theories and actions are opposite to one another. We do not usually go about acting one way, and explaining our actions in the exact opposite way. However, closing the gap between the two theories of action seems a constant pursuit. That is what Ms. Vasquez refers to as the irony of what she stands for and what she at times may say.

In the first sentences of her statement, she alludes to her efforts at self-monitoring. She also suggests how mortifying to her it is to realize that sometimes unwanted expressions may slip through, which, as she puts it, "will project an image of myself that is not who I am." In other words, we may say something that does not reflect both our espoused theories (or ways we explain ourselves) and the image we have of ourselves. The good news is that Ms. Vasquez appears to understand the problem and is willing to wrestle with it. Her willingness suggests that she is making concerted efforts at eliminating the distance between her theory-in-use and her espoused theory.

The second part of Ms. Vasquez's statement uncovers a key element in her progress toward unifying her espoused and in-use theories. When she is unable to "catch" a contradicting utterance, her brother aids her by providing useful and timely feedback. If we were to transfer his role to that of a collective learning endeavor of supportive coworkers, we could argue that applying the critical discourse ideas covered in this book might be not only possible but may also develop a healthier work environment.

In the next section we cover a more elusive type of deficit label: acronyms. These are new words where each letter represents a code, subsequently abstracting multiple meanings at once.

ACRONYMS AS DEEP ABSTRACTIONS

Perhaps the greatest challenge to closing the gap between beliefs and utterances is the use of acronyms as labels. Here is an example:

> A parent wanted her student in RSP classes. I knew the student was capable in a regular classroom. I then explained to this mother that we do modifications on a regular basis in the classroom, [but that] we do this only in case of need. (Rigoberto Palacios, assistant principal, College Academy Middle School)

Rigoberto Palacios was a quiet force in one of the leadership seminars that Gilberto taught. He appeared more comfortable interacting with his school team than with the rest of his peers in the seminar. Yet when he talked to the entire class, he seemed to address issues from convictions cultivated for a long time—and always on the side of equity and justice. At the very end of his first semester of graduate school, his school administrators invited him to compete for an administrative leadership position. After a successful process, he was appointed school assistant principal.

Initially, about ten years earlier, he had gone to college with the idea of becoming a civil engineer—in part because he wanted to work in a similar field to his father (demolition) and in part because he was attracted to problem solving. But things did not work out the way he wanted. His mathematics skills from high school education faltered, and after two years of fruitless efforts, he transferred to social science and eventually to teaching. Yet his unsuccessful attempt at engineering marked Mr. Palacios forever—he wanted to prevent other students from having such experiences due to a lack of college preparation. Today Mr. Palacios cannot conceive of his life outside the field of education.

As assistant principal, he displays tremendous energy and dedication, working with parents whose children end up in his office for misbehaving. Explaining a variety of meanings to both parents and students demands that educators possess a clear knowledge of institutional functions, systems, and regulations. These need to be spelled out in ways that help parents negotiate their relation with schools in advantageous ways.

Mr. Palacios also actively promotes an antilabeling language at his site, yet all of this knowledge and understandings do not always prevent him from employing acronyms as labels. Self-monitoring does help educators eliminate or at least keep in check the use of deficit labels, but as Mr. Palacios statement above suggests, when it comes to acronyms things are more difficult. The reasons for this difficulty have more to do with abstractions and less with intentions.

Let's take a quick pause before we move ahead on acronyms. We have pointed out that a label, in general, abstracts the individual or group thus named. Therefore, this naming takes over social identity. Instead of personalizing the relationship with either individuals or groups, a deficit label such as "at risk" reduces identity to a code representing what is assumed to be wrong about the individual or group. Deficit labeling transforms the subjects into objects and builds social distance between the user of the label and the target person or group. A financial analogy—how we pay for shopping—may further help clarify this point.

Using credit or debit cards—as opposed to currency—has become the primary way most people in the United States pay for shopping. Credit and debit cards make us forget that every time we use them we incur a withdrawal from our checking account or indebt ourselves. When paying with actual money—paper bills or metallic coins that we feel in our hands—the impact on our awareness is immediate and unambiguous. On the other hand, paying with credit cards does not yield texture and immediacy to our transactions. Cards abstract money. Money in turn is an abstraction of labor. So much money represents so many hours of someone's labor. Credit cards operate at a double level of abstraction: We don't see the monetary value of our work, and we lose sight of our indebtedness, doubling the distance between our perceived economic exchange and reality.

Acronyms work in similar ways. They add an extra layer of abstraction to labeling, further distancing us from those abstracted. First of all, when we apply labels—and deficit labels are the worst— we no longer refer to specific, flesh-and-bones individuals who posses personal names and particular faces; we distance ourselves from them by naming them as, say, "at risk" or "resource." Second, when we transform such labels into acronyms, they add extra social distance. Describing a student, for instance, as ADD (attention deficit disorder), triggers in the listener a set of assumptions covering things like short attention span, academic problems, and poor grades. Mr. Palacios, in the excerpt above, runs into this exact situation.

The excerpt suggests that he has few qualms about using an acronym, RSP, which is translated as Resource Specialist Program. The abstraction achieved through using acronyms both normalizes and seems to simplify a complex issue. The acronym constitutes a useful shortcut for speakers and listeners able to decode the meanings. In other words, once an acronym becomes accepted as part of what can be considered "the way we speak here," people apparently have a harder time noticing it, critiquing it, and bringing to mind the entire set of meanings it hides. In much the same way, paying with a credit card distances us from the awareness and possibility of questioning whether we want to spend this much money for a product.

What is true for Mr. Palacios was true for all the study participants: While showing various degrees of awareness about the use of deficit labels, they had a harder time avoiding acronyms. Thus, in the daily vocabulary of these educators, a classroom designated for students with some learning challenges has become RSP, a student learning English, ELD, and a monolingual English speaker, an EO. While some acronyms like ELD are not on the surface deficit labels, they become so in contexts, like California and other states in the nation, where bilingualism is often viewed as a deficit rather than an asset.

TALK STRATEGIES

So far we have shown the meaning of labels and the power deficit labels embody as tools to distort the social world. We have examined the functions of language (i.e. expressive and instrumental) whereby we may at times say things we truly believe in and at other times we may just say things with implications that do not quite mesh with our beliefs. We have looked at how monitoring one's own utterances is a prerequisite to building language substitutions that respond to the uncovering of meanings and/or individuals behind the labels.

We looked at closing the gap between what we do ("in-use" theory) and what we tell others and ourselves we do ("espoused" theory). We closed this section with a discussion about acronyms, as perhaps the most difficult deficit labels to tackle. The following section addresses the most critical challenge: using talk to bring these issues up to the surface.

Educators who addressed deficit labels used a variety of strategies to do so: explaining, interpreting, reframing, and paraphrasing. Chapter 2 describes the strategies of reframing and paraphrasing as general strategies for language intervention. Here we show how they can be applied in the case of deficit labels. Keep in mind that explaining and interpreting, like reframing and paraphrasing, also can be appropriate to any speech situation. Here we illustrate their use in contesting the use of deficit labels.

Explaining and Interpreting

Building a More Complete Picture

As educators know, we truly understand something only if we can explain and interpret it for others. Explaining and interpreting is what we, teachers, do day in and day out in the classroom. We carry these skills everywhere we go in the education system or to other fields, such as business. While they almost always go together, explaining usually means clarifying or shedding light on what is not obvious, whereas interpreting usually means elucidating the instrumental and expressive functions of language such as the effects a label may have on a person's well-being. It is not surprising to find that educators readily turn to these related skills as a means of redressing injustice stemming from deficit labeling.

For example, Jose Jacinto, an assistant principal, tells us how he engages his colleagues at MLK Jr. Middle School.

> I try to let them [teachers] see what I know [about a student being labeled]. I tell them: "Do you know that this student's father was killed in a gang shooting and stuff, that the kid is in a foster home and has nothing, not even uniforms?" I do it when I have an opportunity, when we have a

> conversation. I hope once teachers know about the student they [have labeled], that they will investigate. They usually say, "Oh, I didn't know that."

Mr. Jacinto is a tall, lean, and very assertive young leader of Mexican descent. English is his second language and he reads, writes, and speaks it as well as Spanish. He taught physical education for a long time and decided he needed to work more with adults and the whole school in order to redress the injustices he considered were all too common at his site.

While eagerly seeking to invoke teachers' empathy, Mr. Jacinto intentionally brings up key contextual information to illuminate teachers' perceptions. Instead of indulging in the alienating practices of lecturing or falling into a patronizing behavior, he uses inquiry to stimulate explanations and empathy. He trusts that his questions—as in "Do you know that this student's father . . . ?"—will provoke enough curiosity that the listener will go out and investigate further into the student's life, or that the questions will at least create unsettling feelings that might raise some doubt. Through these follow-up activities, the potential effects of Mr. Jacinto's action could be multiple.

Location and Code-Switching

Ms. Lupe Vasquez raises another important aspect of talk in responding to the question "What do you do when your students use labels against each other?" She explains the function of location and code-switching.

> I know kids use demeaning language in the halls and yards, but once at the threshold of the classroom they don't. They know they cannot. I explain to them that [demeaning language] is a defensive language, and that it's OK to use it in the appropriate place, not in the school. They have to use it to survive in their rough neighborhoods.

Ms. Vasquez first places the use of demeaning language within the needs of street survival—offering in this way a plausible validation to such discursive practice—then she makes a sharp contrast between this context and the context of the classroom. In the street, you must survive; in the classroom, you must learn and show respect and decency. Language, as Ms. Vasquez explains, takes on different meanings and purposes according to place and circumstance.

While in general she may be right in this distinction, demeaning language plays a subordinating function regardless of context. The challenge, therefore, goes beyond distinguishing where and who we speak to. It is, after all, about the use of a language of possibilities that engenders decency, dignity, and respect all the time in all places. For more information on the importance of context, see Chapter 5.

Reframing

Reframing can be used skillfully to identify a speaker's main topic when it is entangled with other topics of lesser importance or is demeaning in some way. Reframing can help the speaker focus the analysis and possible action pertaining to a problem. Reframing can also be used to redirect the topic of conversation so as to illuminate the underlying cultural and social tensions in a particular conversation. The assumption here is that redirecting the topic increases the chance of transforming subordinating language such as labels.

During a social studies department meeting, a group of teachers at Foothill High School is discussing the problems presented by school procedures in regard to student behavior.

Mr. Anton:	You don't refer or expel a student, because it's seen as your failure—that you haven't succeeded in your classroom management. However, a referral helps you control those kids, you know. All discipline problems are problems you resolve in the classroom first, but you must get rid of troublemakers as soon as possible, even if the administration doesn't want to see them at the office.
Ms. Miller:	I have some of those.
Ms. Sandler (teacher-leader):	Have you and other teachers tried to agree on procedure?
Mr. Anton:	We can agree on something general, but it is each one of us who applies the rules according to our own way of managing the class.
Ms. Sandler:	So is the issue one of procedure, or is it one of dealing with "those kids," as you call them?
Mr. Anton:	I guess the latter.
Ms. Sandler:	Help us then understand what you mean by "those kids."

In the situation above, the questions raised by the teacher-leader facilitating the meeting forced Mr. Anton to focus on "those kids," rather than dwelling on procedures or blaming an arguably uncaring administration. The passage shows how the leader reframes the conversation by building on what appears as a legitimate concern to the speaker.

Mr. Anton is apparently ready to move on in the reframed direction, perhaps in part because he knows his point is not being dismissed. The teacher-leader's action sharpened Mr. Anton's communication in its precise intent. Other than venting accumulated frustrations—which at some point may be good to do for therapeutic purposes—this conversation may have produced no positive results if the facilitator hadn't asked the reframing question "is the issue one of procedure or is it one of dealing with 'those kids,' as you call them?"

It is "those kids" who apparently create a challenging classroom environment, not the procedures. The teacher-leader clearly pushes the conversation toward the need to find a topic that might be the source of the challenge for Mr. Anton (and probably Ms. Miller).

Paraphrasing

While reframing is identifying and reorienting a topic (in our case linked to labeling), paraphrasing is about rewording statements for clarity, emphasis, or mutual understanding.

A team of teachers at Solano Middle School—which draws its students from the surrounding neighborhood—is discussing safety issues.

Ms. Brown:	Teachers cannot leave their personal belongings in the portables, cannot stay until too late, and have no hopes for the school security or the administration to help.
Mr. Garcia (facilitator):	Let me see if I understand you correctly. You feel unsafe in your classroom, and the school security and the administration haven't helped.
Ms. Brown:	Yes! You can't depend on anyone else but you, yourself!
Ms. Lightfoot:	Portables were ripped off, before they were installed, while they were installed, and after they were installed.

Mr. Bressi:	Right!! People from the neighborhood steal everything, even water pipes, toilet paper, pens, money, whatever is available.
At this point most participants nod and utter:	Yeah! Yes!
Mr. Garcia:	In other words, the neighbors are the source of your insecurity.
Mr. Bressi:	That's correct!
Ms. Lightfoot:	Yeah! They behave just like their kids do.
Mr. Nguyen:	You can call the school district, and the call gets through, but they never do a thing. There is never an answer to your petition.

In the transcript above, the teacher-leader uses a few key "stem sentences" to clarify the situation and to lead the conversation in what appears a productive direction:

1. Let me see . . .

2. If I understand . . .

3. In other words . . .

Participants in this speech event didn't explicitly use labeling, but as Ms. Lightfoot stated, teachers consider all of the school's neighbors and their children to be thieves. The stem sentences made it possible to restate what the speakers had said so that listeners hear it again, and thus build clarity.

So far we have discussed individual actions only. And at the end of the day, what matters is what individuals do. Yet when a collective group of individuals embrace an action in a systematic and consistent way, the ramifications of such action may be enormous. For instance, when a school celebrates student academic success or behavioral improvement through school assemblies, a sense of fulfillment among students and of efficacy among teachers may ensue. The next section addresses collective action through institutional activities.

INSTITUTIONAL ACTION

Institutional intervention is effective when laws, regulations and, enforcement work consistently together. Institutional action can be a potent modifier of collective social behavior. Antismoking campaigns are a case in point. From the enactment of antitobacco laws in the United States, beginning with the state of Minnesota in the 1970s to this day, smoking in public spaces and the workplace has changed from a cool and sexy habit to an antisocial behavior in most states. Anyone smoking in nondesignated areas meets the ire of collective disapproval. If the violator persists, he will very likely be facing a law enforcement officer.

Similarly, policy and its collective enforcement in schools work effectively in the case of hate language. Teachers and administrators enforce a zero tolerance approach against it. This zero tolerance occurs at the local, state, and national levels. Just take a look at how many radio hosts lost their jobs in the wake of Don Imus and the Rutgers female basketball team incident![4] These events illustrate how we have reached social consensus about the appropriate response to the words and expressions of hate language. Yet building social consensus. by definition, is a contested and changing terrain; today we may use a normalized vocabulary that may become hate language at some point in the future or go the other way around—a concept or expression considered hate language at some point may lose its currency as such and mutate into accepted speech. This is the case of *queer*, which in some dictionaries still appears as offensive language but has become widely adopted in the United States, particularly in university campuses.

The study of the 27 school leaders we have referred to in the earlier sections of this chapter showed us that addressing discourse critically as an institution seems to depend on the existing policies and regulations as well as on the initiative and skill of teachers and administrators. When participants were asked, "What does the school do to redress the use of hate language?" the typical response was, "Follow procedure: write a referral and send the culprit to the assistant principal in charge of discipline."

However, when someone is caught uttering other labels, educators tend to lecture, and punitive measures do not necessarily follow. Study participants explained that in these situations, students needed to have more awareness of (1) the unintended consequences of their speech; (2) the actual meaning of the utterances; and (3) the use of punishment as a last resort.

Let's take an example of a type of label that seems harmless— "school boy." This name sums up a social damnation of those students perceived by their peers as too smart, too studious. What is the intent of this label? We believe it is a device to publicly expose and deride students with outstanding academic achievements so that the collective pressure brings them down to the average.

Students caught in the category of "school boy" determined to resist peer pressure deploy a variety of strategies to avoid what appears to be a harmless label, whether by hiding that they are performing up to their capacity or by finding ways to hide their scores, reading inclinations, and participation. Educators know this problem, and in some cases, they have established a set of ceremonies to counter the negative impact of this label.

Mr. Jacinto, whom we introduced earlier states,

> We give students a block letter, a big M, which is the first initial of our school's name, and then a pin with the sport they play. For academics they get a certificate, for anyone with GPA of 3.0 up. At the end of the year we give the academic recognition; students get a trophy for academic excellence. For those graduating they get a gold cord, specific to our school, representing a 3.5 or higher GPA for all two years. We have 3 assemblies over the year, one a trimester.

Besides these assemblies, educators go out of their way to avoid incurring social pressure. Ms. Pannell, introduced earlier, tells us, "We meet with these *school boys'* parents and give them books to take home for extra work. This way nobody sees the student with more books than regular kids."

Institutional actions aimed at stopping the negative impact of these labels on a culture of academic success often follow an improvised and inconsistent rationale. Other than assemblies, study participants indicated no other activities before or after. School administrators concentrate all resources (e.g., time, professional development) almost exclusively on preparing staff for testing. Thus, as we can glean from the previous sections of this chapter, it is usually up to individual teachers to figure out the best response to deal with the use of seemingly innocuous labels that promote an antilearning climate.

Contractual obligations add an extra layer of difficulty to the issue of institutional redressing of labels. For instance, participants in the study agreed that while teachers may at times have a common prep schedule, teacher are not required to use this time to work together and to engage issues—such as labels. Rather, participants asserted, this time is theirs to do whatever they want to, following the collective labor contract.

So, what can educators do in addition to promoting assemblies? They can engage the institution in systemic, overt, group discussions (e.g., clubs, focus groups, and committees) focused on the dismantling of specific antilearning labels, offensive labels, and hate language. This engagement ought to be done with the clear intent of undermining the negative effects of such language on the school's cultural climate, eventually eradicating them from day-to-day conversation.

One of the things these actions should aim for is the creation of new collective meanings for some of these labels. Similar to what happened to the name "queer" in the United States, as we pointed out, we can stamp out the demeaning and hurtful instrumental use of labels in schools. Labels like "school boy" could then be branded as the "cool thing" to aspire to and that any student would, therefore, be happy to receive.

THOUGHTFUL INACTION

In the previous sections, we have described individual and institutional action. We examined some of the most effective strategies educators deploy in their efforts to redirect talk from deficit labeling to a language of possibilities. What we haven't talked about is what happens if individuals knowingly decide not to act when hearing others use deficit labeling.

The study of the 27 educational leaders indicates that some educators consciously decided not to redress the use of subordinating labels. At times they worried that the power imbalance would render them too vulnerable to (imagined or real) retaliation—that as individuals of a numerical minority (e.g., gender, race/ethnicity, seniority, or language) they would be easily ignored or dismissed—or they simply did not know what to do. Whatever the reasons, while aware of the need to challenge others' discursive practices, they opted to postpone action.

Ms. Vasquez also recalls how she kept her critique to herself at first and only spoke out later as her circumstances changed.

> I didn't engage people at my former school because I was a minority. Now at Hills, it's totally different; the staff is desegregated. We have more Latinos, and I don't feel so alone. In the late 80s using the appropriate language was considered a politically correct thing. So, not saying anything was more to survive in that environment. Nowadays I carefully do it and find people more receptive. Either people have become more tolerant about other races, and in a way more willing to embrace others, or people in schools are more diverse.

Ms. Vasquez's statement suggests a keen understanding of context and risk management. If she had raised questions about language back at her former school, her coworkers probably would have marginalized her. While it is unclear whether she engaged language critically at all in those days, she leaves no doubt that, given the attitudes and demographics of her new school, she does intervene. She no longer considers herself a numerical ethnic minority. Indeed, knowing where she stands—in terms of her relations with others—is a key factor in determining when and how to act.

Knee-jerk reactions[5] are often an ineffective course of action. Our environment plays a big role in our decisions to act or not. (See Chapter 5 for more on this.) Measuring the effects of an action on the listener (e.g., hurting feelings, provoking guilt and shame) is crucial to effective communication. Here we list the three strategic "don'ts":

1. Do not corner the listener to a defensive position.

2. Do not make the listener distrust your motives.

3. Do not invite the listener to frame you as "language police" or as a "politically correct" person.

Last, the force of our language intervention comes from one central point: our will.

> A lot of people feel and are aware of labels, but they're afraid to say anything because they fear the consequences with their peers. Even if they have the skills, it will still be confrontational. They don't have the courage. (Jose Jacinto, assistant principal)

Will here means the energy that propels us to act. Such energy may be the result of a conviction and commitment to confront what we consider unjust and inequitable. Will comes before skill, yet acting without skill leads nowhere. The power of our words is a product of both will and skill.

ACTIVITY: CROWNING WITH DEFICIT LABELS[6]

This activity will help you see how quickly and negatively or positively labels can affect the way you think about yourself and others.

Materials

Have available long strips of fine cardboard in different colors, scissors, markers, glue, staplers, stickers, glitter, and masking tape.

Procedure

Step One: Organize

1. Tell the group they will be divided into three same-size groups.

   a. Group "a" makes crowns and writes a label on front.

   b. Group "b" is crowned by group "a."

   c. Group "c" documents the whole activity.

2. Take group "a" to a different room, and leave the other two groups together.

3. Explain to group "a" that their job is to make crowns and after that they will need to make a list of labels used at their sites. Each participant takes one and writes it down on the front of his/her crown.

Step Two: Get Into Your Positions

1. Once group "a" is ready with their crowns, bring them to where groups "b" and "c" are.

2. Ask group "b" to form a facing-out circle.

3. Ask group "a" to form a facing-in circle surrounding group "b."

4. Ask group "c" to get as close as possible to the double ring circle as observers with notebooks and pens or laptops ready.

Step Three: Do It

1. Repeat directions of interaction: Each member of group "a" crowns a member of group "b." Each member of group "a" then makes a comment to the group "b" member that he or she just crowned; every fifteen seconds group "a" members move clockwise to the next person in the inner circle.

2. The facilitator will let group "a" know when to move by ringing a bell.

3. The exercise ends when each person in group "a" is back to the person in group "b" they faced at the start of the activity.

Step Four: Debrief

1. Ask the whole class to make a large circle around the room.

2. Bring five chairs and make a small circle in the middle of room.

3. One chair is for the facilitator, three for a member of each of the three groups, and one chair remains empty for whoever wants to jump in to the small circle to add, emphasize, or make a comment. This person leaves immediately after their comment, so that the chair is open again to the rest. The facilitator can start the debriefing with questions around form, and then content, from concrete to abstract situations. For instance: How was your experience looking at a colleague in the eye? What were you thinking when you had to remain fixed in your circle? How was it for you expressing ideas about a label you saw on the crown? How did you feel hearing all those things? Were all the labels on the crowns deficit labels or were some innocuous?

4. Participants listening to the debriefing could be assigned the documentation part of the exercise for a later whole group conversation. This documentation could be in the form of field notes, audio taping, or video taping and could be linked to a research project.

CONCLUSION AND SUMMARY OF KEY POINTS

In this chapter we examined the meaning and significance of labels, their contradictions and mutations. Deficit labeling and acronyms perform powerful magical acts in our daily lives—transforming individuals and groups into objects. Rescuing the subject from this object position plays a crucial role in daily communication, and closing the gap between beliefs and actions is but the first hurdle we must deal with.

Summing up, when confronted with an incident involving deficit labels or subordinating language, we identified eight key engagement skills:

1. Monitoring our own utterances and replacing deficit labels with language that places the subject back at the center of discourse

2. Understanding the difference between expressive and instrumental functions of language

3. Recognizing the difference between our theory-in-use and espoused theory

4. Postponing critical engagement of language until the time and place are appropriate, which we call thoughtful inaction

5. Intervening in deficit labeling (and other subordinating language) by using explaining, interpreting, reframing, and paraphrasing skills

6. Understanding the context in terms of things such as race, ethnicity, gender, and seniority before deciding when to intervene

7. Developing institutional means of addressing objectifying language in a consistent, on-going, and forceful manner by the majority of the members of an institution

8. Developing an awareness of your relationship with your colleagues (e.g., knowing how close you are to others), which allows you to find the appropriate moment, place, and tone to critique on language use

Practicing these eight skills will, over time, build a strong cultural context where a language of possibilities will emerge.

NOTES

1. CAHSEE stands for the California High School Exit Exam. To graduate in the state of California, high school students must pass this exam.

2. Troyna and Hatcher (1992).

3. The initial findings of this study were presented at the 2006 American Anthropological Association conference in San Jose, California with the title: "Disrupting discourses of subordination: the ontology of equity." Arriaza (2006, November).

4. For details see Media Matters for America at http://mediamatters .org/items/200704040011 (retrieved September 2008).

5. In Chapter 4 we talked about snap judgments as one type of knee-jerk behavior.

6. This is a modified version of an activity as practiced by Dr. Celestine Villa at the College of Education, San Jose State University (2000).

CHAPTER EIGHT

Conclusion

The Power of Talk

B y now you have learned that both of two seemingly contradictory adages contain a portion of the truth: "Sticks and stones may break my bones, but words will never hurt me," and "The pen is mightier than the sword." Words by themselves will never break your bones, but they can and all too often do help create ways of thinking that would influence someone to believe that breaking your bones is a good idea (e.g., Hitler's rants and Nazi attempts at genocide). But at the same time, we can also use words for transformative purposes. And since words are capable of affecting the way we understand the world, then perhaps the pen (and our spoken or signed words) truly is mightier than the sword.

As you near the end of the book you might ask what this tour of concepts, vignettes, language patterns, and language skills all means. The conclusion is a fitting place to take stock of the variety of topics that we have covered in this book as well as the themes that tie them all together. In addition, you may be wondering, "So now what? How do I use all of this information?" We have shared information and skills relevant to using language that fosters equity and social justice. Social justice does not just magically appear in a school or society; in fact, it is not an end result as much as a process that requires continuing thought, imagination, dialogue, collaboration, and courage.

To that end, we have discussed different ways of thinking about the language we hear and use. We have suggested language patterns that enable imagining and bringing about social justice. We have also suggested some strategies for recognizing and disrupting language use that encourages oppressive ideologies. Although we have covered a wide range of topics, we have by no means exhausted the subject. We have, however, provided some ideas to use as you continue to grow and develop as an educational leader (whether as an administrator, teacher, parent, elected public official, etc.).

School leaders, who help shape the way people (students, teachers, parents, staff, and so on) understand themselves in relation to other people, have far more effect on society than someone wielding a weapon. Thus, if a transformative educational leader wishes to use language as a tool for social justice, they might want to develop an understanding of *the power of talk* in their everyday life. With that thought in mind, we followed three primary objectives in writing this book.

REVISITING THIS BOOK'S OBJECTIVES

We had three objectives concerning the power of language: (1) presenting samples of oppressive and transformative text found in the discourse of educational leaders, (2) offering strategies for speaking transformatively, and (3) providing activities whose purpose is to help leaders develop the skills and awareness necessary for putting their language awareness and transformative strategies into practice. In order for these three objectives to be effectively realized, we also had to introduce and explain key concepts that underlie the use of language as a medium for social change.

To achieve our first objective—presenting samples of oppressive and transformative text found in the discourse of educational leaders—we turned to the actual discourse of educational leaders that we have obtained through our own research. From our observations and interviews with these leaders, we sought three types of discursive patterns: One type promotes oppressive ideologies and acts. The second type effectively engages others to think critically about the way we talk. The third type promotes more equitable ideologies, suggesting a language of possibility.

Our second objective—providing ideas for developing habits and ways of speaking that promote equity and social justice—was achieved through two means. First, we presented the transformative discourses of educational leaders who have struggled (and achieved some success) to develop a climate of possibility within their schools or in larger arenas. These leaders were kind enough to give their time and thoughts to help us learn more about the contexts of their discourse as well as the way they use language transformatively. The other means by which we realized this second objective was through the communication skills we presented in each of the chapters.

The third objective was to provide activities that engage readers in practicing language awareness and developing ways of using language transformatively—the activities in Chapters 3 through 7 can be used by an individual reader, a class, or a group of educators to help make transformative language use part of your everyday repertoire. The introduction of this book suggested some ways this book might be used in a class. The next section elaborates further on how you might use this book in a variety of contexts.

USING THE POWER OF TALK FOR SOCIAL JUSTICE

There are many ways an educational leader, whether a teacher, administrator or parent, can use the information presented in this book. Each chapter is aimed toward helping transform the school community culture into one that more actively fosters social justice. We have written the book so that after reading the first two chapters you can pick and chose which chapters you feel are most important to your community. In the next section, we elaborate three different ways in which this book could be used, starting with a single reader and ending with a more formal institutionalized approach. But in any of these variations (after reading the first two chapters), you can work through the remaining chapters in any order you wish and focus on the ones you feel are most pertinent to your school and community.

Individually

If you have finished reading the book and are wondering how you as an individual can use the book, then we have some suggestions. Our first suggestion is to go back to Chapter 3. First, complete all the activities you can do with just one person. Then for the next two weeks, work on self-monitoring your talk, much like teacher-leader Darbi Pannell, who in Chapter 4 talked about "catching" herself using language that promoted oppressive ideas. As she did, try rephrasing your statements in a way that promotes ideas conducive to a culture of social justice.

When you hear colleagues using othering language, try to follow Edmundo Norte's and others' examples of skillful intervention. Don't try to shame or blame the person for othering someone or a group; simply rephrase the statement in a way that does not other. Another more direct tactic you could try is simply asking questions, for example, "Why did you phrase it that way? How would your meaning be different if you phrased it this way?" Continue this practice with each of the rest of the chapters. There are some activities in some chapters that you will not be able to do as just one person, but you should be able to do most of them.

As you do this, you will not only begin to transform the way you use language in a school context, but you will also begin to change the culture of your school and community. As we discussed in Chapter 7, there may be times when you engage in thoughtful inaction, waiting until a more appropriate time to disrupt talk that promotes negative stereotypes or other forms of inequity. But try to make this an ingrained habit for how you approach your interactions with others and the way you read different texts. It will take a few months, but it is well worth the effort for you and others as you begin to see the world in a new, more hopeful way.

Working With Friends

It may be easier and more fun to work with a buddy. We suggest working with a good friend (or two) who is also interested in using the power of talk to begin creating a more equitable culture and society. Follow the same process, but you can do some of the activities separately and compare results or work together, discussing with each other how best to complete the activities. With just two people, like with one person, there will be a couple of activities that you cannot do. For two weeks you can work not only at monitoring yourselves but also each other. Each of you can begin using the communication skills of rephrasing and questioning with each other and in your school communities to begin transforming the culture there.

Another option, after you have read the book, is to bring it into a more formal institutionalized setting, such as parent-teacher organization (PTO) meetings, as part of faculty development, as a district developmental activity for principals, as part of a workshop for superintendents and/or assistant superintendents, or in a college classroom.

A More Formal Approach

As a member of the PTO, whether a parent or a teacher, you could suggest that all the members who are interested in creating a transformative culture in their school community use the book. PTO members could be asked to read the introduction and Chapters 1 and 2 before the next meeting. At the PTO meeting, people could divide into smaller groups and work on the activities of Chapter 2 and then come together as a large group and compare the small groups' results of those activities.

In the interim before the next meeting, all members can begin monitoring themselves and listening and reading with an awareness of the different ways in which language is used on an everyday basis. Just like the single reader, when members come across othering language, they can rephrase or question that use of language. When doing so, remember to do everything you can to avoid blaming or shaming others. During this same interim members can also read Chapter 3 and repeat the process. Variations of this more formal approach can also be used in faculty inservices or workshops for principals or superintendents.

And finally in a university department of educational leadership, this book could be a requirement for a school reform course. In such a case, the instructor could use it as described above or in a much more condensed manner depending on the length of the course or other instructor objectives.

A FINAL THOUGHT

We would like to revisit the adages mentioned at the beginning of this chapter: "Sticks and stones may break my bones, but words will never hurt me" and "The pen is mightier than the sword." We live in a world and a nation today that has far too much anger, hate, violence, and pain. Key factors leading to negative feelings, thoughts, and actions are a sense of unfairness or injustice and a lack of hope.

We feel pain when we are denigrated implicitly or explicitly through language, and we develop anger when we find that in practice we are denied justice and respect within our schools and society.

These feelings of anger, pain, and hopelessness often lead to hate and violence. And all too often these afflictions are reflected in our society's institutions, such as schools, especially in the communities most besieged by such afflictions. A society saturated with these afflictions often develops a language that reflects them.

This language occurs in our streets and in our schools. As authors, we three often struggled to avoid the metaphors of violence and warfare so prevalent in our schools and in society (e.g., in the trenches, taking aim, tactics, bulwarks). During the process of writing this book, we confronted the difficult task of being critical of the most dominant terminology—that of war and violent sports. And at times, as you no doubt realized while reading the book, we failed.

For example, we hope you noticed the violence of the adages we used to convey the understandings people have about the *power* of language. We recognized this conflict with the way we were using words and our desire to use language that does not normalize violence. So we sought pithy, memorable proverbs that would resonate with people. We were astounded to find that collectively we could not think of any proverbs about the power of language that did not connote violence in some way. Why do you think we failed? We challenge you to think of any pithy, memorable sayings about the power of the word or about power that do not involve violence.

However, things can change for the better, and we can participate in making that change happen. We see a beginning of that change in some of the schools and school leaders that appear in this book. We can help create a society more oriented toward joy, fulfillment, contentment, and justice for all—but it takes thought, work, and courage. By changing the way we talk, we can begin to think and imagine a different way of doing things, a decent and dignifying way of treating people (this includes students) in schools and outside of schools. And we are convinced that almost everyone associated with education, especially educational leaders, *do* want to promote equity and social justice. Writing this book was a learning experience for us. We questioned the language we were using. We found that even as we talked about issues of equity and social justice, we often used language in a way that operated against those values. We began working to transform our own talk (and writing). In other words, being aware of the problem is only half of the job.

We offer this book, *not* as a way of castigating educational leaders, which would only lead to a more negative school and social climate but rather as a way of helping us think about how we actually talk on a day-to-day basis and what to do about it! We believe that in becoming more thoughtful about the ideas we transmit through our talking, educational leaders can begin using language more effectively to promote the ideas and practices of social justice. And a society of social justice and equity is far more likely to be a peaceful, loving, and joyful society than one that acts willingly or unwillingly against such values.

References

Abu El-Haj, T. (2006). *Elusive justice: Wrestling with difference and educational equity in everyday practice.* New York: Routledge.

Alim, H. (2005). Critical language awareness in the United States: Revisiting issues and revising pedagogies in a resegregated society. *Educational Researcher, 34*(7), 24–31.

Allport, G. (1954). *The nature of prejudice.* New York: Perseus Books.

Anyon, J. (1981). Social class and school knowledge. *Curriculum Inquiry 11*(1), 3–42.

Appelbaum, B., & Mellnik T. (2005). Blacks 4 times more likely to pay high rates than whites. *Originator Times.* Retrieved May 25, 2008, from http://originatortimes.com/content/templates/standard.aspx?articleid=452&zoneid=5.

Argyris, C., & Schön, D. (1974). *Theory in practice: Increasing professional effectiveness.* San Francisco: Jossey-Bass.

Arriaza, G., (2006, November). *Disrupting discourses of subordination: The ontology of equity.* Paper presented at the conference of the American Anthropological Association, San Jose, CA.

Arriaza, G., & Arias, A. (1998). Claiming collective memory: Maya languages and civil rights. *Social Justice Journal, 25*(3), 70–79.

Arva, V., & Medgyes, P. (2000). Native and non-native teachers in the classroom. *System, 28,* 355–372.

Bakhtin, M. M. (1982). *The dialogic imagination: Four essays.* Austin: University of Texas Press.

Balibar, E., & Wallerstein, I. (1992). *Race, nation, class: Ambiguous identities.* London: Verso.

Bogdan, R. C., & Biklen, S. K. (1992). *Qualitative research in education: An introduction to theory and methods* (2nd ed.). Boston, MA: Allyn and Bacon.

Bowl, M. (2003). *Non-traditional entrants to higher education: "They talk about people like me."* Stoke on Trent, UK: Trentham Books.

Bowles, S., & Gintis, H. (1976). *Schooling in capitalist America.* New York: Basic Books.

171

Briscoe, F. (2005). A question of representation in educational discourse: Multiplicities and intersections of identities and positionalities. *Educational Studies, 38*(1), 23–41.

Briscoe, F. (2006). Reproduction of racialized hierarchies: Ethnic identities in the discourse of educational leadership. *Journal for Critical Education Policy Studies, 4*(1). Retrieved February 7, 2008, from http://jceps.com/index.php?pageID=article&articleID=60.

Briscoe, F. (2008, March). *The construction of families in the discourse of educational leaders in wealthy and low-wealth school districts: Handicaps and assets.* Presented at the American Association of Applied Linguistics Conference, Washington DC.

Carbó, T. (1997). Who are they? The rhetoric of institutional policies toward the indigenous populations of postrevolutionary Mexico. In S. H. Riggins (Ed.), *The language and politics of exclusion: Others in discourse* (pp. 88–108). Thousand Oaks, CA: Sage Publications.

Creswell, J. W. (2003). *Research design: Qualitative, quantitative and mixed methods.* Thousand Oaks, CA: Sage Publications.

Cuadraz, G. (1993). *Meritocracy unchallenged.* Unpublished doctoral dissertation, University of California, Berkeley.

Darling-Hammond, L. (2007). The flat earth and education: How America's commitment to equity will determine our future. *Educational Researcher, 36*(6), 318–334.

Davis, K., Bazzi, S., Cho, H., Ishida, M., & Soria, J. (2005). It's our "kuleana": A critical participatory approach to language-minority education. In L. Pease-Alvarez & S. Schecter (Eds.), *Learning, teaching, and community: Contributions of situated and participatory approaches to educational innovation* (pp. 3–26). Mahwah, NJ: Lawrence Erlbaum.

De Beauvoir, S. (1973). *The second sex* (E. M. Parshley, Trans.). New York: Vintage. (Original work published 1949)

De Valades, F. (1579). *Rhetorica christiana.* Retrieved December 31, 2007, from http://www.christophebruno.com/2006/10/31/the-web-before-the-web/.

Duzak, A. (2002). Us and others: An introduction. In A. Duzak (Ed.), *Us and others: Social identities across languages, discourses and cultures.* Philadelphia: John Benjamins.

EdSource. Retrieved August 2007 from http://www.edsource.org/pub_cat.cfm.

Education Trust. (2004). *Why we need No Child Left Behind in California. And how on earth does it work?* p. 34. Retrieved August 2007 from http://www2.edtrust.org.

Esling, J. (1998). Everyone has an accent except me. In L. Bauer & P. Trudgill (Eds.), *Language myths* (pp. 169–175). New York: Penguin Books.

Evans, A. (2007). School leaders and their sensemaking about race and demographic change. *Educational Administration Quarterly, 43*(2), 139–188.

Fairclough, N. (1995). *Critical discourse analysis: The critical study of language*. London: Longman Group.

Fairclough, N. (2003). "Political correctness": The politics of culture and language. *Discourse and Society, 14*(1), 17–28.

Flores-González, N. (2002). *School kids/street kids: Identity development in Latino students*. New York: Teacher's College Press.

Friere, P. (1970a). Cultural action and conscientization. *Harvard Educational Review, 40*(3), 452–477.

Friere, P. (1970b). *Pedagogy of the oppressed*. New York: Herder and Herder.

Friere, P. (1993). *Pedagogia da esperança: Um reencontro com a pedagogia do oprimido*. São Paulo Paz e Terra.

Gabbard, D. (2000). *Knowledge and power in the global economy*. New York: Lawrence Erlbaum Publications.

Gardner, H. (1983). *Frames of mind: Multiple intelligences theory*. New York: Basic Books.

Gay, G. (2004). Navigating marginality en route to the professoriate: Graduate students of color learning and living in academia. *International Journal of Qualitative Studies in Education, 17*(2), 265–288.

Gladwell, M. (2005). *Blink: The power of thinking without thinking*. New York: Little Brown.

Gould, J. (1996). *The mismeasure of man*. New York: Norton.

Groopman, J. (2007). *How doctors think*. New York: Houghton Mifflin.

Guilherme, M. (2002). *Critical citizens for an intercultural world: Foreign language education as cultural politics*. Clevedon, England: Multilingual Matters.

Haraway, D. (1991). *Simians, cyborgs, and women: The reinvention of nature*. New York: Routledge.

Harvard Facing History and Ourselves Project. (2002). *Race and membership in American history: The eugenics movement*. Brookline, MA: Facing History and Ourselves National Foundation.

Henze, R. (2005). Metaphors of diversity, intergroup relations, and equity in the discourse of educational leadership. *Journal of Language, Identity, and Education, 4*(4), 243–267.

Henze, R., Katz, A., Norte, E., Sather, S., & Walker, E. (1999). *Leading for diversity: A study of how school leaders achieve racial and ethnic harmony. Final cross-case report*. Oakland, CA: ARC Associates.

Henze, R., Katz, A., Norte, E., Sather, S., & Walker, E. (2002). *Leading for diversity: How school leaders promote positive interethnic relations*. Thousand Oaks, CA: Corwin.

Hernstein, R., & Murray, C. (1994). *The bell curve: Intelligence and class structure in the United States.* Glencoe, Illinois: Free Press.

Holmes, O. W. (1897/2004). *The path of law.* Whitefish, MT: Kessinger.

Johnstone, B. (2008). *Discourse analysis* (2nd ed.). Malden, MA: Blackwell.

Kandel, E. R. (2006). *In search of memory: The emergence of a new science of mind.* New York: Norton.

Kluckhohn, C. (1959). *Mirror for man.* New York: Fawcett.

Kotlowitz, A. (2007, August 5). Our town. *New York Times Magazine,* 31–37, 52, 57.

Kozol, J. (2005). *The shame of the nation: The restoration of apartheid schooling in America.* New York: Crown.

Krovetz, M., & Arriaza, G. (2006). *Collaborative teacher leadership: How teachers can foster equitable schools.* Thousand Oaks, CA: Corwin Press.

Lacan, J. (1977). *Écrits: A selection* (Alan Sheridan, Trans.). New York: Norton.

Lakoff, G. (2004). *Don't think of an elephant.* White River Junction, VT: Chelsea Green.

Lindsay, R. Robins, K., & Terrell, R. (1999). *Cultural proficiency: A manual for school leaders.* Thousand Oaks, CA: Corwin Press.

Loewen, J. (1995). *Lies my teacher told me: Everything your American history textbook got wrong.* New York: Simon & Schuster.

Lorde, Audre. (1984). *Sister outsider: Essays and speeches.* New York: Crossing Press.

Luke, A. (1995). Text and discourse in education: An introduction to critical discourse analysis. In M. Apple (Ed.), *Review of research in education 21* (pp. 3–48). Washington, DC: American Educational Research Association.

Lussier, R., Greenberg, G., & Carmen, J. (1998). Bank financing discrimination against African-American owned small business. *Journal of Business and Entrepreneurship,* Mar 1998. Retrieved on May 25, 2008, from http://findarticles.com/p/articles/mi_qa5424/is_199803/ai_ n21417166.

Markedness. (n.d.). Retrieved Jan. 14, 2008, from http://www.analytictech .com/mb119/markedne.htm.

Martin, D. (1995). The choices of identity. *Social Identities, 1*(1), 5–21.

Marx, K. (1951). The woman question. In K. Marx, F. Engels, V. I. Lenin, & J. Stalin (Eds.), *The woman question: Selections from the writings of Karl Marx, Friedrich Engels, V. I. Lenin, and Joseph Stalin* (pp. 5–37). New York: International.

Miles, M. B., & Huberman, M. (1994). *Qualitative data analysis* (2nd ed.). Thousand Oaks, CA: Sage Publications.

Mukhopadhyay, C., Henze, R., & Moses, Y. (2007). *How real is race? A sourcebook on race, culture, and biology.* Lanham, MD: Rowman & Littlefield Education.

Nanda, S., & Warms, R. (2004). *Cultural anthropology* (8th ed.). Belmont, CA: Wadsworth/Thomson Learning.

National Center for Educational Statistics. (2003). *Status and trends in the education of Hispanics—executive summary.* Retrieved June 16, 2003, from http://nces.ed.gov/pubs2003/hispanics/.

Niemann, Y. (1999). The making of a token: A case study of stereotype threat, stigma, racism, and tokenism in academe. *Frontiers, 20*(1), 111–134.

No Child Left Behind, Public Law 107–110, the No Child Left Behind Act of 2001. Part I, sec. 1903 (a)(2); sec. 1906. Retrieved December 18, 2005, from http://www.ed.gov/policy/elsec/leg/esea02/pg18.html.

North, C. (2006). More than words? Delving into the substantive meaning(s) of "social justice" in education. *Review of Educational Research, 76*(4), 507–535.

Oakes, J. (2005). *Keeping track: How schools structure inequality* (2nd ed.). New Haven, CT: Yale University.

Ogbu, J. (1978). *Minority education and caste: The American system in cross-cultural perspective.* New York: Academic Press.

O'Rourke, M. (2005). Don't let Larry Summers off the hook yet: Why the Harvard president's tactless social science was a bad idea. *The Highbrow: Examining Culture and the Arts.* Retrieved September 2008 from http://www.slate.com/id/2112799/.

Piaget, J. (1954). *The construction of reality in the child.* London: Routledge & Kegan Paul.

Rumberger, R., & Palardy, G. (2005). Does segregation still matter? The impact of student composition on academic achievement in high school. *Teachers College Record, 107*(9), 1999–2045.

Rusch, E. (2004). Gender and race in leadership preparation: A constrained discourse. *Educational Administration Quarterly, 40*(1), 14–46.

Said, E. (1978). *Orientalism: Western conceptions of the Orient.* New York: Pantheon.

Santa Ana, O. (2002). *Brown tide rising: Metaphors of Latinos in contemporary American public discourse.* Austin: University of Texas Press.

Scheurich, J., & Young, M. (1997). Coloring epistemologies: Are our research epistemologies racially biased? *Educational Researcher, 26*(4), 4–16.

Shaw, George Bernard. (1921). *Back to Methuselah.* Part 1, Act 1.

Shi-Xu. (2005). *A cultural approach to discourse.* New York: Palgrave.

Spring, J. (1976). *The sorting machine: National educational policy since 1945.* New York: David McKay.

Spring, J. (2006). *Deculturalization and the struggle for equality: A brief history of the education of dominated cultures in the United States.* New York: McGraw-Hill.

Summers, L. (2005). Letter from President Summers on women and science. *The Office of the President.* Retrieved on April 4, 2008, from http://www.president.harvard.edu/speeches/2005/womensci.html.

Tabakowska, E. (2002). The regime of the other: "Us" and "them" in translation. In A. Duzak (Ed.), *Us and others: Social identities across languages, discourses and cultures.* Philadelphia: John Benjamins.

Texas State Data Center. (2002). Retrieved December 4, 2002, from http://txsdc.tamu.edu/cgiin/htsearch?config=Htdig&restrict=&exclude=&method=and&format=builtinlong&sort=time&matchesperpage10&words=per+capita+income.

Thai, X., & Barrett, T. (2007). Biden's description of Obama draws scrutiny. *CNN Washington Bureau.* Retrieved July 22, 2007, from http://www.cnn.com/2007/POLITICS/01/31/biden.obama/.

Troyna, B., & Hatcher, R. (1992). *Racism in children's lives: A study of mainly-white primary schools.* New York: Routledge.

Valdez, G. (1996). *Con respecto.* New York: Teachers College.

Valenzuela, A. (2005). *Leaving children behind: How "Texas-style" accountability fails Latino youth.* New York: SUNY Press.

Van Dijk, T. (1997). Political discourse and racism: Describing others in Western parliaments. In S. H. Riggins (Ed.), *The language and politics of exclusion: Others in discourse* (pp. 31–64). Thousand Oaks, CA: Sage Publications.

Van Dijk, T. (2001). Critical discourse analysis. In D. Schiffrin, D. Tannen, & H. Hamilton (Eds.), *The handbook of discourse analysis* (pp. 352–371). Malden, MA: Blackwell.

Villenas, S. (2000). This ethnography called my back: Writings of the exotic gaze, 'othering' Latina, and recuperating xicanisma. In E. A. St. Pierre & W. S. Pillow (Eds.), *Working the ruins: Feminist poststructural theory and methods in education* (pp. 74–96). New York: Routledge.

Wink, J. (1997). *Critical pedagogy: Notes from the real world.* New York: Longman.

Index

CORWIN

A SAGE Company

The Corwin logo—a raven striding across an open book—represents the union of courage and learning. Corwin is committed to improving education for all learners by publishing books and other professional development resources for those serving the field of PreK–12 education. By providing practical, hands-on materials, Corwin continues to carry out the promise of its motto: **"Helping Educators Do Their Work Better."**